Mindfulness for Beginners

Declutter your home, body and mind with Essential oils, Hemp Oil and CBD for Pain Management, Natural Remedies and Everyday Meditation Techniques for Anxiety

By

Lauren Marshall

Lauren Marshall

©Copyright 2017 by Lauren Marshall - All rights reserved.

The following eBook is reproduced below with the goal of providing information that is as accurate and reliable as possible. Regardless, purchasing this eBook can be seen as consent to the fact that both the publisher and the author of this book are in no way experts on the topics discussed within and that any recommendations or suggestions that are made herein are for entertainment purposes only. Professionals should be consulted as needed prior to undertaking any of the action endorsed herein.

This declaration is deemed fair and valid by both the American Bar Association and the Committee of Publishers Association and is legally binding throughout the United States.

Furthermore, the transmission, duplication or reproduction of any of the following work including specific information will be considered an illegal act irrespective of if it is done electronically or in print. This extends to creating a secondary or tertiary copy of the work or a recorded copy and is only allowed with express written consent from the Publisher. All additional right reserved.

The information in the following pages is broadly considered to be a truthful and accurate account of facts and as such any inattention, use or misuse of the information in question by the reader will render any resulting actions solely under their purview. There are no scenarios in which the publisher or the original author of this work can be in any fashion deemed liable for any hardship or damages that may befall them after undertaking information described herein.

Additionally, the information in the following pages is intended only for informational purposes and should thus be thought of as universal. As befitting its nature, it is presented without assurance regarding its prolonged validity or interim quality. Trademarks that are mentioned are done without written consent and can in no way be considered an endorsement from the trademark holder.

Medical Disclaimer

This book is not intended as a substitute for the medical advice of physicians. The reader should regularly consult a physician in matters relating to his/her health and particularly with respect to any symptoms that may require diagnosis or medical attention. Any recommendations given in this book are not a substitute for medical advice.

Lauren Marshall

Contents

Introduction: Big Pharma vs Natural Healing 9

Chapter One: Getting to Know Hemp 16

    Why Grow Hemp? 19

    How is CBD Hemp Oil Used? 21

    What are the Potential Side-Effects of CBD Hemp Oil? 21

Chapter Two: Hemp vs Marijuana 23

Chapter Three: Benefits of Hemp Oil and CBD for Physical Injuries & Ailments 28

Chapter Four: Benefits of Hemp Oil and CBD for Mental Health 33

Chapter Five: Benefits of Hemp Oil and CBD Oil for Learning Problems 37

Chapter Six: Benefits of Hemp Oil and CBD Against Aging 40

Chapter Seven: Benefits of Hemp Oil and CBD for Pets 42

    How Can Hemp Oil and CBD Help My Pet? 42

Chapter Eight: Benefits of Hemp Oil and CBD for Fibromyalgia 45

Chapter Nine: Different Types of Hemp CBD Oil 48

    Types of CBD Oil 49

Chapter Ten: User Experiences with CBD Oil 51

    Bi-Polar Disorder 51

    Asperger's Syndrome 52

    Skin Cancer 53

    Schizophrenia 54

    Anorexia 55

Chapter Eleven: How to Use CBD Hemp Oil 58

Chapter Twelve: Guide for Buying CBD Hemp Oil 61

Chapter Thirteen: Growing Cannabis and Making Your Own CBD Hemp Oil at Home 64

    Making Your Own CBD Oil at Home 66

Conclusion 68

Introduction 71

An Overview of Essential Oils 76

Essential Oil Terminology 79

Essential Oils Vs Fragrance Oils and Perfumes - what's the difference? 83

Essential Oils Throughout History 86

Benefits of Aromatherapy 93

The Most Popular Essential Oils 97

Lauren Marshall

Quick Ailment Reference Guide - Which oil to use for which problem 112

Creating Your Own Essential Oil Blends - 22 Super Simple DIY Recipes 116

Conclusion 125

Introduction 127

Chapter One: The Importance of Decluttering and Minimalism 131

    Why Do We Accumulate Clutter? 132

    How Does Clutter Affect Our Health? 135

Chapter Two: Freeing Yourself from Clutter 142

Chapter Three: The Importance of Mindfulness and Meditation 149

    The Three Types of Meditation – And Which One is Right for You 153

    Hidden Benefits of Meditation You Never Knew About 155

    How to meditate, even if you've never done it before in your life... 159

Chapter Four: 8 Exercises for Everyday Mindfulness You Can Do at Home...with no extra cost 166

Other books by Lauren Marshall 172

Lauren Marshall

Hemp Oil and CBD

Your Guide to Using Natural Oils for Physical Injuries, Mental Health & General Wellbeing

By

Lauren Marshall

Introduction: Big Pharma vs Natural Healing

The $450 billion a year pharmaceutical industry is responsible for the creation, distribution and marketing of what is commonly thought of as medicine. Everything from the Aspirin we take to relieve a headache to the Tylenol used to lower a fever qualifies as medicine. Likewise, life-saving drugs such as insulin, epinephrine, Digitalis, as well as penicillin and other vaccines for deadly illnesses fall underneath the blanket term "Big Pharma."

While there are a large number of "Big Pharma" companies in North America, the top three are Johnson and Johnson, Pfizer and Merck and Company.

There are a number of big pharmaceutical companies in America, with the top three being Johnson & Johnson (which did over eighteen billion in sales during the last quarter of 2016), Pfizer (averaged around thirteen billion) and Merck & Company (averaged a relatively minor ten billion in sales).

These three companies are not only incredibly profitable, they are also immensely powerful. They literally hold people's lives and health in their hands, as they control the rights to the medication that these same people need to function from day to day or even to survive. A diabetic must have access to insulin in order to regulate their blood sugar, just as a patient with severe depression may rely upon medication to stabilize their mood swings and control their anxiety. The pharmaceutical companies which manufacture and distribute these medications are able to put a price tag on the health and well-being of other humans. If a person is in need of a certain medication but cannot afford it, the pharmaceutical company does not drop their prices to accommodate the patient's needs. Rather, the patient must find a way to come up with the money needed, or they simply have to go without, often at the detriment of their physical or mental health.

It goes without saying that Big Pharma is an incredibly profitable industry for the key players involved. While the top three pharmaceutical companies did over three trillion dollars' worth of business in 2016 with a profit margin of over twenty percent, it is estimated that seven out of ten drugs released by these companies are too expensive to be realistic for the general population. With the giant profit margins these companies experience, they are facing intense backlash from the average citizen who urges them to drop their prices in order to allow easier access to necessary, life-saving drugs.

So how do they get away with it? Plain and simple, they use the free market and the concept of supply and demand. For example, say a Big Pharma company develops a drug that they know will help save multiple lives and/or improve overall physical health. This product will understandably be in very high demand. The more in demand a product is, the more a company can charge to the consumer. What this unfortunately boils down to, is that the patients who are most in need of a particular medication, such as chemotherapy for cancer treatment, almost always ends up paying far more for their drugs than it actually costs the pharmaceutical company to manufacture and market them.

Not only do Big Pharma companies regularly engage in price gouging and profiteering, there are also serious doubts as to whether or not these pharmaceutical companies are actually working to help improve the health of the citizens they claim to serve. Many companies have been accused of tampering with clinical drug trial results, meaning that they are seeking to emphasize the positive aspects of a certain medication while blatantly glossing over many potentially serious or even fatal side effects that that same drug may carry.

Lauren Marshall

Big Pharma is also responsible for the manufacture and marketing of opioids and other powerful painkillers. Not long ago, these drugs were given freely to patients to treat the physical discomfort associated with recovering from surgery, broken bones, chronic pain issues, etc. While these drugs were certainly effective at relieving pain, they also came with a heavy risk of patient dependency and addiction. The pharmaceutical companies that created these drugs and pushed them upon the general population did not make physicians or patients fully aware of the extreme potential for addiction and resulting health issues. Not surprisingly, this has led to a huge epidemic of opioid addiction in the United States. In fact, opioid addiction numbers have risen a staggering 500% over the past 5 years. This contributes to more than 50,000 deaths per yar among US adults. Many patients who became inadvertently dependent upon prescription drugs following some sort of serious illness or medical crisis, were never properly warned about the potential for developing a chemical dependence upon the drug.

However, recent decades have found many Americans turning away from traditional medicine in an attempt to seek out more natural remedies of maintaining and improving the health. It is not just the fact that Big Pharma so blatantly takes advantage of the same population they claim to serve. Many prescription drugs carry potentially serious side effects or interactions with them that are not experienced with more natural methods of healing.

Many forms of alternative healing, such as aromatherapy, reiki, hypnosis and herbology are finally beginning to make their way into mainstream consciousness rather than being relegated strictly to the realm of new-age hippies. Individuals are finally able to freely access information in order to educate themselves about the various options they have available to them rather than believing they must simply content themselves with following the doctor's orders.

Far and away, one of the most talked about developments in natural healing has been the increased interest in medical marijuana as well as Hemp oil and Cannabidiol, more commonly referred to as CBD. While marijuana, hemp and CBD are all products of the same Cannabis plant, they have very different properties which will be discussed in depth later on in this book. For now, suffice to say that even though Hemp Oil & CBD is far different than marijuana, Big Pharma is very invested in keeping all forms of hemp use illegal, as it profits them greatly to do so.

Lauren Marshall

Pharmaceutical companies are vehemently opposed to legalizing medical marijuana as well conducting research into the effectiveness of CBD hemp oil. This opposition is in the face of a tremendous amount of evidence which shows the beneficial effects that both marijuana and CBD oil possess. Marijuana, for example, has been proven to dramatically improve patient health in instances of Post-Traumatic Stress Disorder, Obsessive Compulsive Disorder as well as with clinical depression. Medical marijuana is a powerful anti-emetic, meaning that it can greatly benefit those with chronic nausea, being particularly effective for patients suffering from the unpleasant side-effects of chemotherapy. Marijuana is also able to stimulate the appetite, which helps patients recovering from anorexia, bulimia or other eating disorders.

CBD hemp oil is being touted by many users as the new "miracle drug" due to its many powerful healing qualities. CBD oil not only helps alleviate seizures, tremors and overall nerve and body pain, it can also calm feelings of anxiety, lessen the symptoms of ADD/ADHD and has even been shown in some studies to decrease or even eliminate the growth of cancer cells and tumors.

This begs the obvious question - if cannabis is so great, then why isn't it legal everywhere? Why don't we have free reign to cultivate, purchase and sell cannabis just as we would any other staple, such as cotton, wheat or soy?

The pure, simply reason as to why Big Pharma fights so mightily against the medical marijuana and hemp industry is not out of concern for the citizens it claims to help. In fact, it is the exact opposite. Big Pharma's resistance towards cannabis is motivated by nothing more than pure, simple monetary motivations. Hemp is relatively easy to grow, meaning that if it were legal, just about anyone in the United States would be able to have unlimited access to the plant. These pharmaceutical companies are very well aware that many patients would turn away from their reliance upon prescription drugs if another viable, legal alternative was made available to them. Thus, Big Pharma continues to block public access to hemp and marijuana out of concern in protecting their own interests. As long as cannabis remains illegal, doctors are forced to stick to prescribing the drugs that the pharmaceutical companies let the prescribe, and Big Pharma keeps on making a ridiculous amount of money off sick Americans each year.

Lauren Marshall

Chapter One: Getting to Know Hemp

Hemp is a variety of Cannabis plant. It is grown strictly for its industrial use, as its fibers have been used to create functional, strong fibers for over ten thousand years. There is a wide variety of things that commercial hemp can be used for, including paper, clothing, rope, sails, textiles, etc.

Hemp has a long, contradictory history in the United States. Beginning in the 1700's, hemp was considered the number one most profitable crop in America. Colonists in Connecticut, Virginia and Massachusetts were required by law to grow hemp on their land, and faced heavy fines and even imprisonment if they neglected to do so. The hemp plant was so valuable during America's colonial days that it could even be exchanged much like money for goods and services.

The cultivation and sale of hemp was completely unregulated until the early 1900's. In 1914, the Harrison Act defined the use of marijuana, and therefore hemp, as a crime. In the next thirteen years, California, Louisiana, New York, Texas and Utah all outlawed marijuana as well. The increasing illegality of cannabis coupled with the invention of the cotton gin in the 1920's caused cotton to quickly replace hemp as the fabric of choice for clothing and textiles.

While the consumption and sale of alcohol became illegal during Prohibition in 1919, Americans were initially encouraged to explore marijuana as a safer alternative, however, once the 1937 Marijuana Tax Act was passed by Congress, all forms of cannabis use became a criminal offense.

Interestingly enough, after the United States was attacked by Japan at Pearl Harbor, signaling the beginning of America's involvement in World War Two, it became extremely difficult to import industrial hemp from countries in eastern Asia. Therefore, the industrial production of hemp was once again not only allowed but in fact heavily encouraged by American farmers, particularly in the Midwest. While hemp cultivation was linked with patriotism for this brief period in time, once the war had ended, so did any legal rights to growing hemp in the United States.

In 1951, the Bogs Act and Narcotic Control Act put the final nail in the coffin of industrial hemp production when the United States Government grouped hemp, marijuana and all other forms of cannabis in together as a singular substance, outlawing all forms for their supposed detrimental effect on the mind and body of those who used them for recreational or therapeutic purposes. By 1957, all forms of industrial hemp was banned in the United States.

While the 1970 Comprehensive Drug Abuse Prevention and Control Act allowed for cannabis to be distinguished from other narcotics such as cocaine due to its marked therapeutic benefits, Regan's 1986 Anti-Drug Abuse Act and subsequent War on Drugs called for mandatory criminal sentences for anyone caught possessing or selling drugs, whether it be marijuana, heroin or another substance.

California is credited with being the first state to legalize cannabis when it was permitted in 1996 for medicinal purposes. The Clinton administration, however, was determined to continue the War on Drugs, and many patients were arrested for imbibing in medical marijuana, as were the physicians who prescribed the treatment. It was not until the Obama administration came onto the scene in 2009 that medicinal use of cannabis was decriminalized, though recreational marijuana use was still considered illegal.

In modern times, the leading world producers of hemp are Canada, France, China and Great Britain. It was not until the year 2014 that hemp farming finally became legal again after Barack Obama passed a law allowing for limited hemp cultivation in the United States. Currently, there are twenty-one states that legally permit hemp growing. They are California, Colorado, Delaware, Hawaii, Illinois, Indiana, Kentucky, Maine, Michigan, Missouri, Montana, Nebraska, New York, North Dakota, Oregon, South Carolina, Tennessee, Utah, Vermont, Washington and West Virginia.

Why Grow Hemp?

Some of the major advantages of growing hemp over other crops are as follows:

Hemp is Super-Strong: Hemp is one of the world's strongest natural fibers, being over ten times stronger than other common fabric materials, such as cotton, nylon, silk or wool. This makes is a useful material for making rope, clothing and other durable goods.

Hemp is Very Diverse, and it Saves A lot of Space: Hemp is a hearty plant, and it can withstand a wide range of temperature and soil conditions. This means that is can be grown in most environments and climates, compared to cotton, which cannot withstand the colder temperatures of the North or the drier conditions of the West. Farmers like hemp because they get a higher return on their initial investment. Compared to cotton or flax, hemp plants can thrive even when they are planted very close together. This allows for a much higher yield per acre.

Hemp Gives a lot Per Individual Plant: As deforestation becomes a very serious issue, hemp is very sustainable as well as profitable. A single acre of hemp is capable of producing up to four times more paper than the wood from an acre of trees. Likewise, hemp grows back many times faster than trees, reaching full maturity within four months instead of a span of multiple years. Hemp is unusual in that is does not exhaust the soil it is grown in or strip it of minerals. Rather, hemp seems to enrich the soil it is grown in, meaning that one farmer could conceivably grow three full, healthy hemp crops each year.

Hemp has a Great Deal of Nutritional and Medicinal Value: Hemp seeds are very high in protein, making them a valuable addition to any idea, yet particularly valuable for vegetarians and vegans. The seeds are also very rich in Vitamin E, which means that they not only benefit the skin but help to strengthen the body's natural immune system as well. The oil produced from hemp, known as CBD hemp oil has a multitude of marked health benefits, including providing relief from seizures, preventing strokes, quelling symptoms of ADD/ADHD and relieving anxiety and depression.

How is CBD Hemp Oil Used?

There are a multitude of methods for using CBD oil, both internally and externally which are discussed in their own separate chapter. However, the most common form of using CBD oil is to consume it sub-lingually in a tincture form, meaning that the drops are administered underneath the tongue. CBD oil may also be made into edibles such as cookies, brownies or candy as well as inhaled through a vaporizer, incorporated into a mouth or nose spray and/or made into a topical lotion, balm or salve.

What are the Potential Side-Effects of CBD Hemp Oil?

Due to the legal issues surrounding cannabis, there is a lack of research on CBD hemp oil as well as medical marijuana. Currently, the Food and Drug Administration classifies it as being possibly safe for adult consumption. Generally speaking, CBD oil is mostly considered to be safe for internal and external use amongst many medical and alternative healing communities, yet there are some potential side effects and interactions associated with its use that must be carefully considered before beginning treatment. Some patients report minor ailments, such as sleeplessness, a feeling of light-headedness and/or diminished saliva production. Some patients also experience issues with lowered blood pressure after taking CBD oil as well. Some doctors caution patients to avoid ingesting grapefruit juice while undergoing CBD hemp oil treatment as well.

Patient's with Parkinson's Disease are warned to avoid using CBD hemp oil, as it is theorized that it may actual make tremors and shaking worse. Additionally, it is important that pregnant women abstain from all forms of CBD Hemp oil use as well. Those women who are in the progress of nursing a child should avoid use as well, along with babies and infants. Small children may benefit from low dosages of CBD oil, though it is absolutely vital that the lowest possible effective dose is used, and that the child's progress is monitored by a qualified medical professional.

Chapter Two: Hemp vs Marijuana

Many people mistakenly believe that hemp and marijuana are the same thing. Given the history, it is easy to see why the confusion is so common, seeing that they have often been treated as the same substance by the United States government. While both hemp and marijuana come from the Cannabis plant, there are a multitude of differences between the two. Cannabis itself is one of the oldest domesticated crops in the United States, having been cultivated by such great historical figures as George Washington, John Adams and Thomas Jefferson. In fact, the Declaration of Independence, which is often considered to be the most defining document in American history was printed on paper derived from the cannabis plant!

So what is the difference?

The leaves and flowering tops of the cannabis plant contain what is known as tetrahydrocannabinol, more commonly referred to as THC. These are the only parts of the cannabis plant that contain psychoactive properties, and thus, they are harvested, dried and smoked or made into edibles for their mind-altering and therapeutic effects. THC is what makes a person feel high or "stoned" after smoking or consuming marijuana. The higher the concentration of THC in a particularly cannabis plant, the stronger the psychoactive effect is on the user.

Hemp, on the other hand, comes from the seeds and stalks of the cannabis plant rather than the buds. This part of the plant contains a very miniscule amount of THC, which makes it useless for any kind of recreational drug use. Hemp instead has very highly concentrated levels of something called cannabidiol, which is more commonly referred to as CBD Hemp oil.

Generally speaking, marijuana plants are smaller and bushier than hemp plants. Marijuana is more difficult to grow as well, as it is far fussier than its cousin, relying upon ample sunlight and plenty of growing space to ensure proper flowering and multiple buds. Marijuana farmers are concerned with maximizing THC content and care only about cultivating the buds or flowering tops of the plant, while those growing hemp are concerned with strengthening the cannabis' stalk.

To put the difference between marijuana and hemp into perspective, the average strain of marijuana boasts about fourteen to twenty percent THC. However, in order to classify as hemp instead of marijuana, cannabis must be an absolute maximum of one percent THC, though levels as low as 0.03 percent are standard in Colorado and other states.

Not only is there a big difference between marijuana and hemp, there is also a difference between hemp oil and CBD Hemp oil. Hemp oil is produced solely from the seeds, and acts as a natural demulcent and emollient for the skin. This makes it a popular addition to moisturizers, lip balms, lotions and other cosmetics. CBD Hemp oil, however, is more commonly used for medicinal and/or therapeutic purposes. While hemp oil contains zero THC, CBD Hemp oil does contain trace amounts, **though not enough to stimulate any psychoactive effects.** To reiterate, CBD has no psychoactive properties.

Let's Talk Legalities

Ok, so you're probably wondering if you'll get "high" while taking Hemp Oil or CBD. While the FDA currently groups marijuana and hemp together under the category of cannabis, the simple fact is that hemp contains absolutely zero psychoactive or mind-altering properties.

Therefore no matter how much hemp or CBD Hemp oil a patient consumes or inhales, they will not get high or feel "stoned."

States That Have Legalized Industrial Hemp Production

- Alabama, Arkansas, California, Colorado, Florida, Georgia, Hawaii, Illinois, Indiana, Kentucky, Maine, Michigan, Minnesota, Mississippi, Montana, Nebraska, Nevada, New Hampshire, North Carolina, North Dakota, Oregon, Pennsylvania, Rhode Island, South Carolina, Tennessee, Utah, Vermont, Virginia, Washington and Wyoming.

States That Have Legalized Hemp Oil/CBD Hemp Oil

- Legal in all fifty states, though CBD Hemp oil is still illegal in Idaho, Indiana, Kansas, Nebraska, South Dakota and West Virginia.

States That Have Legalized Medicinal Marijuana

- Alaska, Arizona, Arkansas, California, Colorado, Connecticut, Delaware, Florida, Hawaii, Illinois, Maine, Maryland, Massachusetts, Michigan, Minnesota, Montana, Nevada, New Hampshire, New Jersey, New Mexico, New York, North Dakota, Ohio, Oregon, Pennsylvania, Rhode Island,

Vermont, Washington, Washington DC and West Virginia.

States That Have Legalized Recreational Use of Marijuana

- Alaska, California, Colorado, Maine, Massachusetts, Nevada, Oregon and Washington.

Chapter Three: Benefits of Hemp Oil and CBD for Physical Injuries & Ailments

CBD Hemp oil does not contain a high enough level of THC to produce any kind of psychoactive effect on those who use it. Thus, individuals who utilize CBD Hemp oil as a component in a therapeutic regimen will not experience any mind-altering side effects, but will still reap the medicinal benefits.

The human body has an endocannabinoid system which includes receptors all over the body. CBD Hemp oil, like all other cannabinoids attaches itself to these receptors, of which there are two kinds. CBD1 receptors are mostly located in the brain, and these are also the receptors that are most highly affected by the presence of THC. CBD2 receptors are located throughout the entire body, yet rather than being connected with the brain, they are connected to the immune system. CBD Hemp oil works by stimulating the body's CBD2 receptors, helping to fight off and prevent diseases.

CBD Hemp oil has been shown to have a dramatic effect upon a number of physical ailments, such as

Multiple Sclerosis: Commonly referred to as MS, Multiple Sclerosis causes miscommunication in the nerves, meaning that signals between the brain and body are often askew. Patients may suffer from an inability to move their arms or legs, blindness or compromised vision, uncontrollable shaking as well as a feeling of electricity that passes through the neck.

CBD hemp oil is being shown to provide relief to MS patients. It can help reduce pain levels as well as quell body tremors. Multiple sclerosis often interferes with its victims' sleep patterns, and CBD hemp oil can also be useful for promoting sleep.

Recommendation: Multiple sclerosis is best treated with CBD oil strains that carry a high CBD level, such as Charlotte's Web or Sour Tsunami.

Diabetes: Diabetes is a disease which is characterized by the body's inability to produce enough insulin. Insulin production is what regulates the body's blood sugar or glucose level. There are two types of diabetes. In type one diabetics, the body has a problem making insulin, while in those with type two, the body does not properly utilize the insulin it makes.

Over 30 million Americans are diabetic. Complications from the disease can result in neuropathy and nerve damage in the feet and hands as well as damage to the eyes, kidneys and cardiovascular system.

Studies conducted at the Hebrew University of Jerusalem suggest that CBD oil's ability to reduce inflammation may stabilize the metabolism of those who suffer from type two diabetes. Diabetics can also benefit from CBD hemp oil's ability to reduce the neuropathy in the fingertips and toes

There is some research that suggests that using CBD oil can actually prevent diabetes by improving fasting blood sugar levels and combatting obesity, which is one of the leading causes of Type II diabetes. However, there are only limited resources for this topic, so it should strictly be considered a theory at this point in time.

Alzheimer's Disease: Alzheimer's Disease is characterized by the onset of dementia which progresses over time. Symptoms of dementia include confusion, loss in short and long-term memory, changes in mood and difficulty problem solving and/or completing everyday tasks.

Alzheimer's Disease is a terrifying diagnosis. The memory gradually decreases until patients are unable to recognize the people around them. Patients with moderate to advanced Alzheimer's Disease may find themselves suddenly confused as to their location or the period of time they are living in. This can understandably cause these patients to experience moments of panic or aggression towards their surroundings.

There is some research demonstrating that small amounts of THC can slow the production of beta-amyloid proteins, which are a key factor in the progression of the disease. Both the American Journal of Alzheimer's Disease and the Salk Institute have research on this topic. There is also evidence of CBD's usefulness in helping to stabilize the mood swings and wandering that are so characteristic of the illness.

Epilepsy: Epilepsy is a neurological condition that is characterized by the sudden onset of seizures that do not have another underlying cause. In order for a person to be diagnosed as an epileptic, they must have experienced at least two unexplained seizures.

CBD oil can be used to help epileptics control their seizures. While epilepsy cannot be cured, CBD oil is effective at lessening the time and intensity of the convulsive episodes. A 2017 study by the New England Journal of Medicine found a 23% decrease in seizures among child epilepsy patients taking CBD oil when compared to those taking a placebo. In fact, there is evidence that cannabis and its derivatives have been used to treat epilepsy since the 1800s. It is a particularly valuable alternative for doctors who are hesitant to increase the dosage in patients receiving traditional seizure drugs with major side effects.

Cancer: Cancer is basically the renegade mutation of cells in the body. The cancer cells reproduce rapidly and attack healthy cells. There has been a great deal of excitement emerging over the pronounced effect that CBD oil has on these cancer cells. Not only does CBD oil appear to prevent cancer cells from spreading throughout the body, it also attacks active cancer cells.

CBD oil has been shown to improve patient prognosis in a number of cancers, including brain, breast, colon, lung, prostate as well as leukemia. CBD oil is thought of in many circles as being the miracle cure for cancer that doctors and rest of modern medicine has been seeking for years.

Research by the American Association of Cancer Research has shown that Cannabinoids can be useful in the treatment of prostate cancer. A study by the Journal of Neurochemistry on mice found that CBD helped reduced cancer growth rates within test subjects.

Chapter Four: Benefits of Hemp Oil and CBD for Mental Health

Treating mental health disorders is one of the absolute biggest money makers for the pharmaceutical companies. Patients who suffer from anxiety, depression, obsessive-compulsive disorder, manic depression and post-traumatic stress disorder are given a cocktail of different medications which simultaneously dull their symptoms as well as their personalities.

Each separate disorder has a multitude of pills currently available on the market which are geared towards alleviating the symptoms. Aside from causing feelings of general disconnection from the rest of the world and chronic fatigue, many of these medications carry very potentially serious side effects and actually cause dependency upon the medication.

For example, Zoloft and Lexapro are two of the most commonly prescribed medications for treating clinical depression. Depression is a very common mental health disorder which varies in its severity which results from a chemical imbalance in the brain. While the above medications help to correct this imbalance, both also carry with them the risk of causing tremors, agitation and even seizures in their users.

A panic disorder is characterized by the sudden onset of intense fear. These panic attacks may or may not be caused by an external trigger, such as a certain noise or smell. Patients with a pronounced panic disorder can have difficulty completing day to day activities, as their irrational fears may prevent them from engaging in simple tasks, such as socializing with others. Alprazolam and Lorazepam are both proven to help with the symptoms of anxiety, yet these drugs are also extremely addictive, and the patient may quickly build a tolerance to them, leading to a need for an increased dosage. Patients may also suffer from major withdrawal and even death if they are to stop taking these medications suddenly, as the body becomes dependent upon them.

CBD hemp oil is being slowly recognized for its ability to effectively treat many forms of mental illnesses and psychiatric disorders. While it does provide relief for the symptoms patients experience, it is particularly valuable because unlike its Big Pharma counterparts, CBD oil is able to provide results without the risk of major side effects or forming an addiction.

First and foremost, CBD oil is a very powerful anti-psychotic. This means that administering a few drops underneath the tongue of a patient who is undergoing some sort of mental crisis has an almost instantaneously calming, soothing effect, thereby working to de-escalate the initial crisis.

Patients who suffer from schizophrenia often report the presence of auditory and even physical hallucinations. They may hear voices speaking to them in an empty room, or may see the presence of people who are not really there. Schizophrenics are often unable to truly determine what is real and what is a product of the disease, and can become easily agitated, combative or even violent. CBD oil has shown to help decrease these hallucinations as well as to stabilize the mood in patients with schizophrenia. A 2011 study in Schizophrenia Research showed that CBD was associated with significantly lower degrees of psychotic symptoms. The two authors of the study T.A. Iseger and M.G. Bassong went on to conclude that the studies "further confirm the potential of CBD as an effective, safe and well-tolerated antipsychotic compound"

Another mental disorder which benefits from CBD oil is post-traumatic stress disorder. Particularly prevalent amongst veterans and trauma survivors, PTSD is characterized by the sudden onset of flashbacks, in which the patient is transported back in their mind to a traumatic moment in their personal history. For a veteran, they may feel as though they are back on the battlefield after hearing a firework discharge, whereas an abuse survivor may have a flashback triggered by hearing a man yell loudly across the street.

CBD oil has shown promise in helping to reduce the frequency of these flashbacks by lowering the initial anxiety levels in patients with PTSD. Unlike the traditional medications which are usually prescribed for PTSD, CBD oil helps promote a feeling of calm without dulling the other senses.

Chapter Five: Benefits of Hemp Oil and CBD Oil for Learning Problems

It is not only physical and mental illnesses that can be beneficially treated with CBD hemp oil. Studies have shown the drug to be tremendously effective for patients who are diagnosed with a broad spectrum of learning disabilities, including ADD/ADHD and those who fall on the autism spectrum.

ADD (Attention Deficit Disorder) and ADHD (Attention Deficit Hyperactivity Disorder) are commonly diagnosed in children around the age of seven or eight, and symptoms may disappear with age or present themselves throughout a lifetime. ADD/ADHD is a very common disorder which is characterized by an inability to focus and concentrate on the task at hand. Oftentimes, students with ADD/ADHD may seem as though they are constantly fidgeting or otherwise goofing off, yet this is not due to an intentional rebellion but rather the fact that their brains simply handle a lack of stimulation far worse than others. ADD/ADHD students are often highly intelligent, yet they may fall behind in their classes due to an inability to focus long enough to express aptitude in any subject.

People who suffer from ADD/ADHA often have very low levels of dopamine in their brains. As dopamine is the chemical which is responsible for causing feelings of happiness and contentment, these individuals who lack the chemical can suffer from inexplicable bouts of anger and irritability. Hemp oil and CBD help provide increased dopamine to the brain, which helps reduce aggression in ADD/ADHD patients.

Another learning disorder which seems to benefit from CBD hemp oil treatment is autism and Asperger's disease. While many people mistakenly believe they are the same ailment, there are some key differences:

Autism Spectrum Disorders are characterized by issues with communication and socializing. The symptoms of autism vary considerably from one person to another. Those who have a mild case of autism may experience difficulty interacting with others, preferring instead to fixate intently on certain areas of life, such as a particular school subject or hobby. On the more extreme end of the autism spectrum, patients may be completely non-verbal and dependent upon help from others to complete basic day to day tasks, such as dressing, feeding or washing oneself.

Asperger's Disease is a form of high-functioning autism. While many who fall along the autism spectrum experience marked developmental delays, those with Asperger's typically have an IQ that is on par with or superior to their peers. They do, however, experience difficulty with socializing, and may have trouble making eye contact, feeling empathy for others or engage in repetitive actions or movements, such as rocking, counting, moving objects, etc.

CBD oil has been shown to help alleviate some of the most problematic symptoms of autism and Asperger's. Studies including those in Current Neuropharmacology suggest that CBD oil not only helps to alleviate the obsessive tendencies which are common to both disorders, it also decreases levels of anxiety, thus allowing the individual to relax in social situations. CBD oil is also helpful for stabilizing the mood swings and bouts of aggression which can result from frustration at not being able to effectively communicate.

Lauren Marshall

Chapter Six: Benefits of Hemp Oil and CBD Against Aging

The skin is the largest organ on the human body. As we age, the collagen in our skin begins to break down, which leads to wrinkles, fine lines and other signs of aging. There are a multitude of environmental factors which accelerate visible signs of aging in the skin, such as smoking, sun exposure and the pollution levels in the air.

Hemp oil and CBD are incredibly beneficial to the skin. CBD oil is a powerful antioxidant that can combat the effects of aging better that Vitamin E or C. The topical application of hemp oil causes the CBD to be absorbed quickly through the skin cells, as the cannabinoid receptors highly concentrated here. The oil not only helps to protect against the harmful UV rays from the sun, it also forms a shield between the skin and any free radicals that may be present within an environment. A study in Swiss research paper Molecules confirmed CBD's antioxidant and anti-aging properties.

One of the largest factors that contributes to aged skin is a lack of moisture. Hemp oil is a common addition to many salves, balms and lotions for its ability to quench the skin's thirst without leaving behind a residue.

Aside from toll that aging can take on the skin, it can also wreak havoc on maintaining a sleep schedule. Most people need anywhere from six to nine hours of sleep a night, with the need being greater in infancy and less in older age. Disruptions in sleep as well as general insomnia are an unfortunate side effect of getting older, and a consistent lack of sleep can lead to health issues as well as agitation. Hemp oil and CBD is highly effective at promoting a regular sleep cycle in individuals of all ages, yet it is particularly valuable for helping to alleviate insomnia in patients over sixty years old.

Chapter Seven: Benefits of Hemp Oil and CBD for Pets

It is not only humans that reap the benefits of hemp oil and CBD, it has also been proven to have a number of beneficial effects on domestic pets, such as cats and dogs. In recent years, studies have been carried out specifically on dogs to prove the effectiveness of CBD in small doses. Previously, owners were self-dosing dogs and cats with human grade edible marijuana, which is not safe. However, pioneering studies by Veterinarians at Colorado State University have allowed us to determine safe levels of CBD oil for pets. When taken in appropriate dosages (a general rule of thumb is to administer one milligram per ten pounds of body weight), CBD helps alleviate many behavioral problems as well as alleviating symptoms of physical diseases.

How Can Hemp Oil and CBD Help My Pet?

Hemp oil and CBD have a marked calming effect

Some animals are simply higher strung by nature than others. Cats or dogs who have been rescued from an abusive or neglectful situation may suffer from a form of animal post-traumatic stress disorder which causes anxiety and even flashbacks. Even if they have been raised in a loving environment from day one, animals with a nervous temperament are more prone to obsessive tendencies and anxious behavior. This anxiety can manifest in a number of undesirable ways, from chewing/clawing furniture to urinating/defecating in in appropriate areas or even outright biting and scratching.

Even animals that are not prone to anxiety may experience intense fear when exposed to loud noises, such as thunder, gun shots or hammering. Hemp oil and CBD is effective in helping to calm these fears by stimulating the brain's natural supply of cannabinoids. This provides a sense of calmness and an increase in endorphins, which eliminates the feeling of panic and danger.

CBD is valuable for pain management

CBD oil not only helps eliminate nervous energy in dogs and cats, it can also assist with relieving symptoms associated with old age, such as arthritis. CBD oil can combat the inflammation in the joints which causes the pain associated with arthritis, and may also be able to help preserve vision and prevent cataracts.

Animals who undergo surgery can benefit from CBD oil as well, as it helps lower pain levels without affecting respiration or consciousness. Likewise, CBD oil promotes restfulness, which helps provide a serene environment that helps with speeding along the recovery process after an accident or surgery by promoting a calming mindset that emphasizes relaxation and rest. Hemp oil and CBD is also effective at helping to treat physical discomfort associated with cancer and other diseases in domestic dogs and cats.

CBD helps prevent symptoms of aging

A regular regimen of CBD hemp oil helps to prevent against arthritis, stiff joints, loss of appetite, lethargy and other common symptoms of aging in mature dogs and cats. Regular administration of CBD assists with maintaining brain health as well.

Chapter Eight: Benefits of Hemp Oil and CBD for Fibromyalgia

Fibromyalgia is a disease characterized by moderate to intense nerve pain known as neuropathy. This pain can seem to radiate throughout the whole body, though medical tests may show no concrete reason for the discomfort. Patients with fibromyalgia may suffer from what appears to be phantom pain, meaning that there is no viable explanation for what is actually hurting. These pains are often widespread and chronic, occurring over the entire body for up to four months at a time. No one is entirely sure what causes fibromyalgia, though it is markedly more common in women than men. While there is no known cure, patients are able to control their symptoms with a variety of medications.

The most common prescription medications for fibromyalgia are Lyrica, Cymbalta and Neurontin. All of these drugs are certainly effective in relieving the nerve pain associated with fibromyalgia, yet all carry some very serious potential side effects and interactions.

Lyrica: (Pregabalin) Minor side effects include vertigo, dry mouth, limb swelling and weight gain, while serious side effects range from extreme fatigue, blurred vision and even potential major kidney damage. In some patients, Lyrica can cause aggression and suicidal tendencies as well.

Cymbalta: (Duloxetine) Some of Cymbalta's minor side effects are nausea, constipation or fatigue. Like Lyrica, Cymbalta has been known to cause extreme, dangerous mood shifts in some patients which can result in extreme aggression or suicide if not immediately treated. Another potentially serious side effect of Cymbalta is uncontrolled muscle stiffness and/or seizure activity.

Neurontin: (Gabapentin) While Neurontin is most commonly used to control seizure activity in epileptics, it does help to relieve symptoms of fibromyalgia as well. Less serious side effects include fatigue and a lowered immune system, however Neurontin can also uncontrolled eye movement as well as changes in behavior and mood. Some may find that their mood swings are amplified and far more intense, while others may experience severe depression and/or anger.

The commonly prescribed medications for fibromyalgia are valuable in that they certainly provide the patient with relief from the nerve pain which is the hallmark of the disease. However, these drugs all carry with them very serious side effects, most remarkably on the detrimental effect they can have on the patient's mental health.

Hemp oil and CBD have not been proven in any official medical studies to alleviate the pain associated with fibromyalgia, yet there is a large population of patients who are urging the medical community to do more research on this topic. Many victims of fibromyalgia stop taking their medication due to an inability to tolerate the drug's side effects. CBD oil shows remarkable potential for alleviating the symptoms without any of the potentially dangerous psychological side effects.

Chapter Nine: Different Types of Hemp CBD Oil

Hemp Oil

There are two primary forms of hemp oils. Hemp seed oil is either unrefined or refined. Unrefined hemp oil is cold pressed, meaning that there is very minimum heat used when extracting the oil from the cannabis plant, which means that it retains the majority of its nutritional and anti-oxidant properties. Refined hemp oil is nature's equivalent of bleached flour. Virtually all of the nutritional and therapeutic properties have been lost in the refining process, though the oil is still good for topical use, such as making soaps and/or moisturizers.

CBD Hemp Oil

CBD hemp oil is entirely different. It is a cannabinoid that is extracted from the hemp plant. While it affects the cannabinoid receptors in the brain, it does not contain any psychoactive properties, which means that it does not get its users "high", no matter if it is smoked, consumed or applied topically.

Types of CBD Oil

Rick Simpson Oil

One of the most popular forms of CBD oil is Rick Simpson Oil, which was concocted by the medical marijuana pioneer and activist of the same name. After Simpson used this particular concentration of oil to cure himself from skin cancer over ten years ago, he was determined to bring his message of alternative healing to the greater population. Unlike CBD oil, Rick Simpson oil contains THC as well, which can be undesirable for some patients. The Indica strains of Rick Simpson oil are used to treat physical ailments, while sativa strains have proven to work well on patients with anxiety, PTSD and other mental ailments. While the oil is available for purchase online, albeit illegally, those in need of its benefits are able to create the medicine in their own homes by following Simpson's detailed online instructions, as long as all necessary safety precautions are taken. These instructions can be found at www.phoenixtears.ca

High CBD Cannabis Strains

CBD oil is made out of cannabis which contains high levels of CBD rather than THC. This means that while the psychoactive properties are non-existent, the healing properties of the cannabis plant are magnified. The top strains of CBD oil that have the highest levels of CBD are Charlotte's Web, Harlequin, Sour Tsunami and Cannatonic.

Chapter Ten: User Experiences with CBD Oil

CBD oil users of all ages and backgrounds have a forum to share their experiences and suggestions with one another at www.420evaluationsonline.com.

Bi-Polar Disorder

While there is a plethora of first- hand accounts which illustrate the various ways in which CBD oil's valuable healing properties have improved the lives of countless individuals, one of the most moving accounts comes from a young man named Casey who suffers from manic depression, otherwise known as bi-polar disorder. Casey states that he even though he knew he was sick, he refused to go on medicine for years because he was afraid of the potential side effects. While Casey shunned the thought of drugging himself into a stupor with traditional medications, he began doing research on his own, and came across a website that advertised the benefits of utilizing CBD as an alternative to psychotropic drugs.

Casey's mood swings had increased in intensity along with his anxiety to the point where he decided he had nothing to lose by giving CBD oil a try After only two weeks of using CBD oil, he reports a dramatic decrease in his symptoms, to the point where he is able to go to work "for the first time in ten years without having anxiety."

Asperger's Syndrome

A woman named Adrienne reports that she was initially hesitant to explore CBD oil, mistakenly believing that it was the same as marijuana. However, after she continued to read more information, Adrienne and her husband made the decision to purchase CBD oil in an attempt to help their son, who suffers from Asperger's Syndrome, relieve his social anxiety. Adrienne conducted a series of tests, all which proved to her and her family beyond a shadow of a doubt that CBD oil was invaluable for helping their son live his life as normally as possible. For example, Adrienne states that her son fixated on all kinds of sports, and was previously easily thrown into hysterics by any sort of change to his expected routine.

One day, her son got the time wrong for his sport's camp, and instead of becoming agitated and going into a full-blown anxiety attack, he was able to simply place a calm phone call to his mother asking that she come pick him up. It is not only the couple's son that has benefited from CBD oil.

Adrienne's husband uses the oil for its ability to relieve digestive issues as well as for nausea and vertigo associated with motion sickness.

Skin Cancer

Of course, no chapter dedicated to CBD oil user's experiences would be complete without discussing Rick Simpson. A film producer who is a major advocate for the legalization of marijuana and all hemp production, his film *Run from the Cure* expresses his dismay at the advantage the pharmaceutical company has over patients with cancer. Simpson in fact claims that CBD oil can be used to cure many forms of carcinoma, as it did with his own skin cancer.

It is not only Rick Simpson who advocates for CBD oil's cancer curing properties. A woman named Sharon Kelly was diagnosed with Stage four small-cell lung cancer which had spread to the lymph nodes and stomach. Her prognosis was considered terminal, and she was given less than a year to live. After all attempts at chemo failed, Kelly's daughter began to research CBD oil on the internet, and was encouraged by what she saw. Figuring that she may be able to buy herself more time, Kelly began using CBD suppositories. Only seven months after beginning daily CBD oil treatment, not only had Kelly's tumors shrunk, they had completely disappeared! Her doctors were absolutely baffled by the fact that she has remained cancer-free for over one year!

Schizophrenia

A teenage girl by the name of Stephanie credits CBD oil with saving her life. Diagnosed as a paranoid schizophrenic at the age of sixteen, Stephanie suffered from regular bouts of intense auditory and sensory hallucinations, where she would hear voices instructing her to hurt herself and the people around her, as well as a pervasive sensation of being scratched, pinched and touched.

Stephanie began receiving intense psychiatric treatment shortly after being diagnosed. In addition to intense therapy, she was prescribed no less than seven different medications to take each day, along with two other PRN meds which were provided in case of a psychotic break or extreme episode.

Stephanie faithfully took her medicine and adhered to her therapy schedule. While the intensity and frequency of her schizophrenic symptoms was alleviated by the medicine, she also experienced a dramatic decrease in energy. She reports that not only was she sleepy and foggy-brained most of the time, she also began to experience a general feeling of isolation from the general world, leading to thoughts of suicide.

Stephanie began undergoing CBD oil treatment about five months ago, and reports a dramatic change not only in her symptoms but in her overall quality of life as well. Not only have the hallucinations drastically reduced, she has an increase in energy which allows her to get back out in the world and participate in the activities she had previously shunned. "I still have to take medicine, but its only one pill a day instead of a handful," she says. "The CBD oil is the best thing I could have done. It has literally saved my life."

Further evidence of CBD's effectiveness in treating schizophrenia is evident on the reddit schizophrenia forum. With users citing "CBD made the voices stop" and "I have been using CBD oil … for a few months now. It works well. For me, the symptoms of schizophrenia are still there, but lessened."

Anorexia

A young woman who suffered from anorexia for over three years finally found relief in CBD oil treatment. Twenty-three year old Katrina states that she began developing an eating disorder back at the tender age of fourteen, when she first auditioned for her high school cheerleading team. "I was told to come back next year after I'd lost ten pounds," Katrina recalls. "I was about five and a half feet tall, and weighed one hundred and fifteen pounds. I was by no mean fat, or even large. But those words stuck in my head for the rest of my life."

Katrina suffered from anorexia and bulimia for the next three years, at one point weighing in at a mere eighty-nine pounds. She began to develop cardiac issues, as well as alopecia and dental issues.

Katrina underwent intense psychotherapy for her eating disorder, yet it is the introduction of CBD oil that she credits with helping her the most. "My aunt had done a lot of research on it," she says. 'And we gave it a try." CBD oil makes it possible for Katrina to concentrate on the pleasures of life rather than living in a constant state of anxiety.

Pain Management

The Washington Post covered a story which illustrated medical marijuana and CBD oil's benefits for athletes, particularly those who formerly played for the NFL. Some retired players, such as Ebenezer Ekuban sustained injuries during the course of their career that left them with chronic aches and pains ranging from moderate to severe. While such conditions can be treated with a range of prescription pain killers, many former athletes are weary of the potential side effects and addictive nature of these drugs.

CBD oil has been proven to be a valuable part of pain prevention in individuals who suffer from sports related injuries. Steve Foley, who played in the league for 7 years is another former NFL player who utilizes CBD oil as a part of his healing regime, both for pain prevention as well as for help with sleep.

Chapter Eleven: How to Use CBD Hemp Oil

CBD hemp oil takes on different forms, depending upon the individual's preference. Generally available for purchase online as well as in state approved cannabis dispensaries, the recommended dosage is listed on the outside of the product. While there is no definitive dosage that is considered ideal, patients who are new to using CBD oil are encouraged to start with a very small dose that is gradually increased in order to find the right dose for the individual. Finding the ideal dose of CBD can be difficult, and requires time and documentation. One may have to gradually increase and subsequently decrease the dose until the desired results are achieved.

CBD oil is most common inhaled or ingested, though there are other methods of administering. Some of the most common methods of using CBD oil are listed below:

Tincture: This means that the CBD oil has been extracted and combined with alcohol as a solvent. CBD hemp oil tinctures are taken orally, usually by placing underneath the tongue, and come with a dropper that helps calculate dosage. It is important to be sure to shake the tincture thoroughly before each use, as natural separation can occur.

Vaporize: CBD oil can be smoked in a vaporizer, though this method is said to be less effective than ingesting it orally. A vaporizer is simply a tool which heats up the oil, causing it to take on a smoke form that is subsequently inhaled.

Concentrate: A concentrate is usually the strongest dosage of CBD currently available on the market. While these concentrates are administered under the tongue in a manner similar to a tincture, and are far more potent, they also lack any outside flavoring, which can cause some to turn away from them. The taste of raw CBD oil is somewhat bitter and not entirely palatable, which is why it is often combined with other more pleasing elements before ingestion.

Capsules: This form works well for people who do not desire to taste any kind of the CBD oil. These gelatin capsules contain anywhere from 5 to 20 milligrams of CBD apiece, thus it is very easy to keep track of the exact amount entering one's system. The precise dosage of capsules allows patients to more accurately adjust their dosage until they are able to find one that works best for them.

Sprays: CBD Hemp Oil sprays typically have the lowest concentration of CBD, and are therefore generally safer for children and the elderly. In addition to being highly portable, the spray is far more convenient for many people than a tincture or concentrate. CBD oil sprays are typically combined with other natural flavors to improve their taste and appeal.

Balms or Salves: Topical use of CBD hemp oil is effective at softening the skin and reducing visible signs of aging along with having the added benefit of relieving pain in the muscles and joints. Overexposure to the sun can cause extreme pain and subdermal damage, and studies have suggested that applying CBD or hemp oil to the exposed area can lessen the intensity of the burn while also preventing against blistering and peeling.

Chapter Twelve: Guide for Buying CBD Hemp Oil

Hemp oil is legal and permitted for use throughout the entirety of the United States. CBD oil however, is a different matter. As mentioned before, there are still six states which consider hemp and CBD to be no different than marijuana, thus it is still classified as an illegal narcotic, even for medical reasons. These are Idaho, South Dakota, Nebraska, Kansas, Indiana and West Virginia.

In the other forty-four states, the use of CBD oil is legal to treat specific medical conditions, such as epilepsy, cancer, schizophrenia, fibromyalgia, ADD/ADHD, Alzheimer's Disease, etc.

While CBD oil can be purchased in state regulated dispensaries in places where medicinal and recreational marijuana has been legalized, those who live in locations which still prohibit cannabis can gain access to CBD oil by utilizing the internet. There is a wide variety of websites offering various strains of CBD oil at a relatively reasonable price. Provided that one is over the age of eighteen, CBD oil can be purchased by anyone online who has a valid credit card or debit card.

Even major distributors such as Wal-Mart, Target and CVS are exploring the hemp oil and CBD market. Some of the most reputable online places for purchasing CBD oil include NuLeaf and Bluebird.

Unfortunately, CBD oil can be relatively expensive, costing up to sixty dollars for 120 ml, and it is important to consider quality over other more budget friendly options. Even though products with a higher cannabidiol content are more expensive, they also work better with a lower dosage, thus making a better investment per gram than oils with lower levels of cannabidiol.

How to Dose CBD Oil

As with anything, if you haven't tried CBD oil before, it's best to start small. The wonderful thing about CBD oil is that it's easy to increase the dosage by a few mg at a time.

The following is a rough guide for CBD dosing for various ailments. Once again, this is a guide and will vary from person to person - so start small

To increase appetite in cancer patients: 2.5 milligrams of THC by mouth with or without 1 mg of CBD for six weeks

To relieve chronic pain: 2.5-20 mg CBD by mouth for an average of 25 days

To treat epilepsy: 200-300 mg of CBD by mouth daily for up to 4.5 months

To treat movement problems associated with Huntington's disease: 10 mg per kilogram of CBD by mouth daily for six weeks

To regulate sleep disorders: 40-160 mg CBD by mouth.

To treat multiple sclerosis symptoms: Cannabis plant extracts containing 2.5-120 milligrams of a THC-CBD combination by mouth daily for 2-15 weeks. A mouth spray might contain 2.7 milligrams of THC and 2.5 milligrams of CBD at doses of 2.5-120 milligram for up to eight weeks. Patients typically use eight sprays within any three hours, with a maximum of 48 sprays in any 24-hour period.

To treat schizophrenia: 40-1,280 mg CBD by mouth daily for up to four weeks

To treat glaucoma: a single CBD dose of 20-40 mg under the tongue. Doses greater than 40 mg may actually increase eye pressure.

Chapter Thirteen: Growing Cannabis and Making Your Own CBD Hemp Oil at Home

In spite of the recent influx in patients utilizing cannabis for medical and mental health reasons, there are only a certain number of states which allow for the private cultivation of cannabis in any form. Be sure to review the beginning pages of this document for more information on where your own state stands on growing cannabis and making CBD oil.

Most states that allow for legalized marijuana also permit people to grow their own cannabis at home, though the exact number of mature plants permitted per person varies from state to state. In places that have only legalized medicinal marijuana, one must have a doctor's prescription to grow or possess cannabis, though in some cases, a "caretaker" can be nominated. This means that someone other than the patient is legally allowed to grow their supply of cannabis for them, even though the caretaker may not have a legal prescription for marijuana.

Those wishing to cultivate cannabis at home must first start with seeds and a grow room. The quality of the seeds determines the quality of the cannabis, so it is advisable to either purchase seeds from a reputable source or use ones that have previously produced a successful crop.

Having an area of the home specifically designated to the growth of cannabis plants ensures that the amount of light and moisture the plants are exposed to during the growth phase is consistent and easy to alter. Likewise, growing indoors helps prevent against environmental obstacles, such as a drastic drop in temperature or hungry insects which may destroy the crop overnight.

Growing cannabis requires that the growing environment be kept just right. Oftentimes, the lights are put on a timer to ensure that each plant does not receive too little or too much sunlight. Likewise, a constant air flow must be present to allow for proper ventilation. The temperature must be regulated as well, and kept between sixty and eighty-five degrees.

Most cannabis growers cultivate marijuana in soil, yet some prefer to work with hydroponics. In this method, the nutrients that would normally be absorbed through the soil instead go directly to the plants roots via osmosis.

Making Your Own CBD Oil at Home

The first step is selecting the marijuana to use for supplying the oil. Usually anywhere from a quarter to a half an ounce is sufficient. The buds from the cannabis must be chopped finely, or shredded in an herb grinder.

The shredded herb is then placed in a sealed glass mason jar with a cup of extra virgin olive oil or coconut oil and gently shaken before heating the mixture in approximately 200 degree water for between three to four hours. The mixture is then left to cool, then heated in the same way again and cooled before being strained through cheesecloth and set aside for use. The concentration of cannabinoids in the solution is increased with each heating/cooling cycle, so the oil can be tailored to individual use and preference.

The resulting CBD oil should be stored in glass jars in a cool, dry place away from direct sunlight. The mixture should keep at maximum potency for approximately four to six months. When considering making your own CBD oil at home, be sure to consult the precise legal status and regulations regarding your particular state.

Conclusion

We have explored just about every aspect of cannabis and hemp in this manuscript. Perhaps no other plant on the planet is as controversial as the cannabis plant. It has been alternately vilified as a dangerous drug in such cult classic movies as Reefer Madness and heralded as a miracle cure for a variety of physical and mental ailments.

The bottom line is that there are some very obvious healing properties associated with cannabis, whether it is in the form of marijuana or CBD hemp oil. In spite of whatever personal feelings one may have against cannabis, the magnitude of its positive effect in medical and therapeutic cases cannot be simply dismissed.

What does the future hold for cannabis? Many states continue to actively campaign for legalized marijuana, especially after seeing proof with other states such as Colorado that recreational legalization not only can work, it generates a great deal of profitable revenue for the state as well.

CBD hemp oil is gaining recognition for its tremendous healing properties. There is absolutely no question that CBD oil helps to treat the symptoms of different diseases as effectively or more than the drugs which are administered by pharmaceutical companies. As cannabis becomes de-mystified and de-vilified by moving into realm of public research and knowledge, we may find that the answer to combatting physical and mental health issues lies in researching what nature has already provided for us rather than trying to synthesize a cure.

Essential Oils

Discover the Drug-Free, Safe & Inexpensive Way to Combat Anxiety & Stress with 20 DIY Recipes

By

Lauren Marshal

Introduction

As little as a few decades ago, essential oils were not very popular in mainstream western culture. Although many different cultures throughout history have utilized essential oils for medicinal and spiritual purposes, much of the knowledge regarding their value was lost. Instead, the subject was deemed a new-age fad, relegated to the same territory as astrology, fortune telling and reading auras. It was not until the end of the twenty-first century that we began to see a renewed interest in the subject. Today, aromatherapy is a reputable subject for practice and study, and essential oils are readily available. You can find them not only in specialty stores geared towards natural healing, but also in major drugstore and on line as well!

It may be difficult for those who are unfamiliar with the subject to believe that essential oils and aromatherapy actual have any true healing properties. Yet, even the most skeptical critic cannot deny the how influential our sense of smell is. Certain smells can trigger memories better than any of our other senses, and these smells also have a marked effect on our mood and state of mind. For example, many people associate the smell of fresh cut grass with summertime. Exposure to the scent triggers receptors in the brain that increase happiness and promote a relaxed, carefree feeling, much as we used to experience during the long warm days of our childhood. Likewise, certain smells may carry negative connotations for certain people. As an example, the smell of gasoline may trigger anxiety and even outright panic in people who have been involved in car accidents.

It is not only the way that smells affect our mood and mental state that makes aromatherapy such an interesting discipline. Certain essential oils also carry some very valid healing qualities. Citrus oils are remarkably stimulating and can assist with elevating energy levels while also increasing the immune system. Tea tree oil is excellent for discouraging ticks and biting insects, while peppermint oil discourages mice and spiders from taking up residence in an area. Lavender oil has been proven to drastically reduce the intensity of migraine headaches, while chamomile oil is wonderful for combatting insomnia and night terrors.

Essential oils are also utilized in many different beauty products. For example, even the most exclusive, pricy designer perfumes are basically composed of one or more essential oils which have been diluted with water. Likewise, a huge amount of personal care items ranging from very expensive to remarkably cheap use essential oils for fragrance and therapeutic benefits. These include soaps, lotions, shampoos, bath bombs, etc. Some companies elect to use fragrance oils instead of essential oils, which means the consumer receives the aromatic smell of the plant but reaps none of the healing benefits.

Historically, essential oils were used out of sheer practicality as well as for their value in medicine, ceremony and spiritual areas. In the days before we had access to flush toilets, running water, refrigeration and other modern conveniences, living conditions were often less than sanitary. Human waste was collected in chamber pots and tossed out into the street, and as there was no garbage man who made the rounds weekly, rotting produce and other waste was often left in the streets to fester. In some areas that were particularly hard hit with plague and other diseases, corpses could be left in piles before they were able to be buried in a mass grave or burned. As one might expect, the result was a powerfully unpleasant smell that permeated the air, as well as an infestation of fleas, rats and other pests running rampant, leading to prime conditions for the farther spread of disease.

Essential oils were not only valued for their ability to cover up the worst of the horrific smell, some were also used for their anti-septic and anti-biotic qualities, as well as for their ability to keep disease spreading pests at bay.

In modern times, we utilize essential oils for cosmetic reasons as well as for the benefits they provide for the mind, body and soul. While essential oils are readily available and anyone can choose to purchase and work with them, it is very important to have a basic working knowledge as to what essential oils are, and what they can and cannot do before beginning to use them. There are definite risks and potentially negative side effects which can occur if you carelessly experiment without knowing what you are doing. As we will discuss more in depth later on, the essential oil market is not very well regulated. In fact, the Food and Drug Administration does not even have a precise definition for essential oils, instead treating them exactly the same as the plant source they came from. The FDA also does not distinguish between essential oils and fragrance oils, so it is very important to know exactly what you are looking for and read the labels before making a purchase. The way that companies advertise is not heavily regulated either. This means that manufacturers can put labels on their bottles which sound appealing and make them stand out from other selections, yet in reality, the terms they use don't really mean anything at all.

    The aim of this book is to provide the reader with a basic introduction to essential oils and aromatherapy. Here, you will learn about the benefits as well as the potential risks associated with certain oils, as well as exploring the most popular oils available for purchase today. You will even learn how to create your own essential oil blends to tailor them to your exact need, as well as receiving instruction on how to properly store them for maximum longevity.

Essential oils are wonderful to experiment with once you know what you are doing, so be sure to take the time to educate yourself about each and every oil you choose to utilize. This book will provide you with a basic overview, yet it is necessary to keep in mind that there may be potential risks associated with particular oils that are not specifically covered here. In regards to children and animals, it is always better to be safe than sorry and store the essential oils well out of reach. If your are pregnant or nursing, be sure to consult with your doctor before using any kind of essential oil internally, externally or aromatically.

Lauren Marshall

An Overview of Essential Oils

So what exactly are essential oils? This is a question that can be very confusing for someone who is just beginning to explore the subject, as there is no precise definition. The best way to describe an essential oil is to say that it is a super-concentrated form of a specific plant. Each and every plant contains natural oils within it. These natural oils are in place to create a natural barrier against potential predators and diseases. Because these oils protect the plant, they are necessary, or essential to the vitality of the plant's life. As long the oils are in place, the plant generally remains healthy and unharmed. These oils are found in the plant's blossoms, leaves, bark, resin and roots, and they constitute the major component of essential oils.

When you pick a lavender blossom, you can certainly inhale the scent and derive some of the plant's aromatic gifts. However, a small bottle of lavender essential oil is the end the result of a significant amount of the blossoms which have been condensed into a singular, powerful oil. In the process of becoming an essential oil, everything that is not therapeutic has been removed from the lavender, leaving you only with the parts that have medicinal and spiritual value. Essential oils are far more potent than a plant in its natural form. In fact, many times, a singular drop is enough to produce results! Peppermint oil is another good example.

While you can certainly gather fresh or dried peppermint leaves and leave them in the corners of your home to discourage mice and spiders, you can achieve even better results with just a drop or two of the essential oil on a cotton ball!

When you look at a cedar tree, it is difficult to understand how that giant tree could possibly wind up in a small bottle that can be carried around in the pocket. The process of extracting essential oils from the raw plants is something that typically occurs via two different methods – steam distillation and mechanical expression.

Steam distillations uses super-heated steam to release the oils from their protective sacs within the plant. The heat from the steam forces its way through the tiny pores in the plant and collects the oils with it as it passes through. The steam turns into water in a condensation chamber, and the oils rise to the top of the mixture, allowing for easy collection.

Mechanical expression, on the other hand, uses gravity rather than heat for extraction. Essential oils that are obtained via mechanical expression rather than steam distillation may also be referred to as cold pressed. Instead of collection the oils via the use of extreme temperatures, they are instead literally pressed out of the plant via the use of tremendous force and gravitational pull.

Lauren Marshall

    The vast majority of essential oils you can find available for purchase are obtained via steam distillation. While this is by far the more common of the two extraction methods, the exception to the rule is in regards to essential oils which are obtained from citrus fruit. Wild orange, grapefruit, lemon and lime oils are all derived via mechanical expression, as the oil comes from applying force to the rind rather than any part of the plant that could be easily distilled.

Essential Oil Terminology

Particularly when you are just beginning to learn about and work with essential oils, choosing the right ones can be confusing at best and completely overwhelming at worst. There are a number of different brands and varieties to choose from, and it is very important to be aware that some of these companies will intentionally try to market their essential oils with clever wording and flashy labels to make their product appear to be superior to the competition.

In the process of exploring your choices, you may come across certain bottles of essential oils which carry a label which reads "therapeutic grade." Although the terminology sounds good and may even initially convince you that this particular oil choice is stronger, purer or more valuable for health benefits and aromatherapy purposes, the reality is that the therapeutic grade label means absolutely nothing. This is certainly not to say that the essential oil in question is inferior to other products, it just means that it is not necessarily any better either.

There is no precise or defined set of guidelines in place that deals with regulating different grades and qualities of essential oils. In fact, there is very little regulation in place regarding essential oils in general, as the FDA labels them both a cosmetic and a drug and makes decisions on a case by case basis. As there is no true regulation, the term therapeutic grade is rendered null and void, as any company can elect to use that wording, regardless of their qualifications. It is simply a label that is freely put on the bottle to make the product appear more attractive to the customer rather than a term that carries any kind of true significance.

You will also come across essential oils that are labeled pure vs blended. Here, those two terms definitely do mean two separate and distinct products, and the difference is exactly what it sounds like. An essential oil that is labeled one hundred percent pure means that that bottle of oil contains the oils of only one plant species, while a blend is made up of anywhere from one to many different essential oils. For example, if you are exploring essential oils to assist with a lack of energy, you may elect to purchase a bottle of one essential oil that carries a strong reputation for increasing vitality, such as peppermint, lemon or eucalyptus. However, you may also choose to purchase a pre-blended bottle of oil that contains all three of these individual oils which is specifically geared towards combatting lethargy.

So, is it better to work with pure essential oils, or blended oils? As with everything, there are distinct advantages and setbacks associated with both.

Pure oils are nice to work with because you know exactly what you are getting every time. If you are electing to utilize an essential oil for a particular need, it is important to use a product that contains that oil and that oil only. For example, tea tree oil is very beneficial for the skin, and has the ability to repel insects and ticks. This makes tea tree oil an ideal choice for hikers and those who spend a lot of time outdoors. Pure tea tree oil can be applied to the skin and generally tolerated without any major irritation, however, if you were to apply a blend of tea tree and lemon to your skin, the risks of obtaining a severe sunburn are substantial, as the addition of lemon oil results in heightened photosensitivity.

Anyone who crafts their own essential oil blends must begin with pure oils as a basic stepping stone. If you buy a bottle of pure lavender oil, you can build your own blends precisely to achieve the results you want, whereas if you are trying to work with a lavender blend, there are variables in your recipe that you may be unaware of. Unless you have created the blended oil yourself, it is virtually impossible to be confident of the exact contents.

Blended oils certainly have their advantages as well. While some people may take great delight in concocting their own special blends, others may be interested in utilizing essential oils, but do not have the time or finances to explore each oil individually. Instead of purchasing three or four separate oils and blending them together in precise proportions, it is far more convenient to buy one professionally preblended oil that is specifically geared towards a specific purpose, such as alleviating anxiety or promoting focus and concentration. Those with a busy, on-the-go lifestyle are particularly drawn to essential oil blends, as they can simply place a few drops of one oil into their diffuser and walk away rather than concocting a specialized formula each day.

    Aside from convenience, blended oils tend to have the financial edge. Pure essential oils require a large number of raw plant material to produce a small amount of oil. The extraction process can be quite tedious and long, which is why some essential oils, such as neroli and tuberose are extremely expensive in their pure form yet become significantly more affordable when added to a blend.

Essential Oils Vs Fragrance Oils and Perfumes - what's the difference?

It can be very confusing to try and distinguish the key difference essential oils and fragrance oils. While some may presume that essential oils are what give a scented candle or air freshener its appealing smell, this is not always true. Oftentimes, these products obtain their scent from synthetic fragrance oils rather than essential oils, which means that the aroma is created in a laboratory rather than in nature. This is the primary difference between essential oils and fragrance oils – one is one hundred percent natural, while the other is not. As a result, the scent you will obtain from product which incorporates lavender fragrance oil may smell exactly the same as products which utilize pure lavender oil, yet in contrast to the pure form, the synthetic version will supply zero health or therapeutic benefits. A bar of soap containing actual lavender oil will not only soften the skin and sooth sunburn, it will contribute a sense of tranquility to the bathing process as well. While lavender soaps scented with synthetic fragrance oils may still provide the appealing smell, the therapeutic benefits do not exist.

Perfumes are created in a laboratory while essential oils are created by mother nature. Synthetic perfume oils serve one purpose, and one purpose only. This is to create a smell which appealing to the human nose. Some designer labels demand upwards of hundreds of dollars for a small bottle of their signature perfume, yet in making this purchase, the customer is paying for sheer smell alone. There are absolutely zero therapeutic benefits associated with even the priciest, most exclusive synthetic fragrance. Even though these companies may advertise that they contain beneficial scents, such as jasmine, lavender or ylang-ylang, these scents are not derived from a natural source, meaning they are not the same.

Not only do synthetic perfume oils tend to be far more expensive than essential oil blends with a similar fragrance, the perfume oil scent is diluted with water or alcohol. Not only does this mean that the fragrance will evaporate from the skin in much less time, it also can leave the skin dried out and irritated from the alcohol.

Essential oils can be applied to the pulse points of the body, such as the inner wrists, inside of the knees and along the throat one time per day, and the scent will continue to be noticeable. Because the oil is super-concentrated rather than diluted, it is long lasting. This means that you not only have to apply your fragrance less often, it means that you use less product, which ultimately saves on money.

Some people have respiratory issues and/or allergies that result in an extreme adverse reaction to synthetic perfume oils. These same individuals are also usually able to tolerate using essential oils, as the natural compounds are not as irritating to the lungs as the synthetic product. This is particularly true in the case of scented candles, air fresheners and other products that rely upon synthetic perfume oils rather than essential oils for fragrance. Not only do these products not carry any therapeutic benefits, even though their label may imply otherwise, they may actually cause harm, as they are essentially diffusing chemicals throughout the area they are used in.

It does bear mentioning that many essential oils are extremely irritating to the skin when applied directly out of the bottle. It is therefore always necessary to utilize a good, quality carrier oil (more on this later) to help create a boundary between the essential oil and the skin. It is also a good idea to do your research beforehand regarding any oil you plan on using. Some essential oils, such as orange, lemon and cinnamon are extremely reactive to sunlight, so you definitely don't want to be wearing them if you're planning on spending the day at the beach or hitting up the tanning bed. As a general precaution, it is always wise to do an allergy/irritant spot test on a very small area of skin before working with the oil.

Lauren Marshall

Essential Oils Throughout History

China: Nature and the natural world has always figured heavily into traditional Chinese medicine; therefore, it comes as no surprise that China is currently one of the biggest exporters of essential oils in the entire world! Chinese medicine uses essential oils for therapeutic ailments. Traditionally, Chinese aromatherapy involves the combination of three separate fragrances, which serve as a top, base and middle note. The top, or high note is intended to disappear quickly, while the middle notes last around eight hours. The base note, however, is the most enduring, in some cases lasting up to two days! Three separate oils may be combined to combat a psychological, spiritual or physical ailment, or simply one may be used, depending upon the situation. For example, a simple top note of something citrus, such as lemon or orange may be all that is needed to restore vitality, while those with chronic fatigue may require the three-fold blend, consisting of a citrus top note and longer acting middle and base notes.

In Chinese culture, any essential oil is believed to be infused with the essence or raw life force of the plant it came from. This essence is called *jing*, and it is a very powerful component in achieving balance between the heart, mind, body and soul as well as for healing a variety of physical and mental ailments. Essential oils are frequently used in conjunction with acupuncture, another ancient form of Chinese medicine that involves stimulating various areas of the body via the insertion of tiny, thin needles.

Egypt: Research shows that essential oils were being used in Egypt as early as 4500 BC! In fact, during ancient Egypt's heyday, you had to be a priest or someone of tremendous spiritual significance in order to work firsthand with essential oils. These oils were considered to be gifts from the gods, and they were therefore too valuable and too sacred to be entrusted in the hands of everyday people. Thus, they were given to those who were seen as being closet to the Gods. The priests were educated in the subject and could distribute the oils accordingly to those who they determined were in need of them, yet they alone had the privilege and/or knowledge of mixing and storing the oils.

The ancient Egyptians were a deeply spiritual culture. They attributed magical qualities to everything from certain animals, such as cats and crocodiles to various plants that were used for ceremonial purposes as well as healing. The ancient Egyptians are responsible for the creation of Kyphi, a blend of over sixteen essential oils that was used in the temples for its extreme spiritual value. Various deities, such as Bastet, Ra and Osiris had their own sacred essential oil blends which were used in ceremony to invoke their favor by anointing their statues. Each Pharo was considered to be an embodiment of the divine, thus they all had their own select blends of oils which were specifically created for them by the priests. These oils were used for many different purposes, depending upon the need at the time. Some would use their oil blend to anoint their weapons before going into battle with the enemy, while others would sprinkle the oil upon their bedsheets to improve their virility and to encourage healthy heirs.

The benefits of essential oils were not only limited to the priests and pharos, however. Cleopatra herself was said to be a huge fan of essential oils from a very young age. She reportedly had a number of blends crafted for her which she regularly used for everything from enhancing her legendary beauty to seducing potential suitors to granting protection from the evil eye.

Greek/Roman: Ancient Greek/Roman culture heavily incorporated essential oils into their everyday lives as well as utilizing them for ceremonial and other spiritual purposes. Certain blends were used to anoint and perfume the body to grant protection and increase bravery before going into battle, while other oils were incorporated into massages and baths to promote relaxation and to increase morale.

Hippocrates was an ancient Greek physician who lived from 460 – 370 BC. If you're not already familiar with his work, he was often referred to as the Father of Modern Medicine, each and every physician must agree to abide by the Hippocratic Oath before commencing practice, meaning that they agree to adhere to a basic code of ethical conduct when they agree to take on the title of doctor. Hippocrates was a strong advocate for aromatherapy or using essential oils for a therapeutic purpose. In order to live a long, healthy live, he believed that every person should indulge daily in an aromatic bath followed by a rigorous massage which also incorporated essential oils.

It is believed that the Greeks were one of the first cultures to begin documenting written knowledge of essential oils, though most of this knowledge was taken from Egyptian culture.

India: The form of healing that was practiced in ancient India is typically referred to as Ayurveda. Ayurvedic medicine is one of the oldest documented medicinal systems in the entire world, originating sometime well over three thousand years ago! The system is centered around the concept of chakras, which are particular areas in the body where energy tends to concentrate. Different essential oils are known to have an effect on different chakras, making them a valuable addition to reiki, meditation and other practices which rely upon balancing the energy of a person's chakras.

- **The Root Chakra:** Located at the base of the spine, this is the chakra that rules over our basic sense of security and belonging in the world. Root chakra work responds to essential oils that are grounding and earth-based in nature, such as patchouli or myrrh.
- **The Sacral Chakra:** Located just below the belly button, this is the chakra that rules over our sense of sexuality, sensuality, passion and creativity. The sacral chakra responds to essential oils that have an aphrodisiac, libido enhancing quality, such as ylang-ylang and sandalwood.
- **The Solar Plexus Chakra:** This is the warrior chakra, the part of our body that determines energy, self-esteem and confidence in our interactions with the world. Working with this chakra requires the ability to honest evaluate oneself, as one may need more cooling or heating oils, depending upon the state of being. For example, if you are a person who tend to have difficulty speaking up for yourself, you may want to concentrate on more stimulating, fiery oils such as cinnamon or black pepper while those who have trouble keeping their tempers in check may benefit from a more soothing, cooling oil such as wintergreen or eucalyptus. Both oils stimulate the chakra, just in a different way.
- **The Heart Chakra:** Located at the heart, this is the center of emotion in the body. Stimulating the heart

chakra promotes romance and a relief from anxiety and depression, while the solar plexus chakra regulates the sexual aspects of a relationship. The heart chakra is what binds us to the people we love, as well as that which gives us the strength to endure uncomfortable emotions, such as fear and depression. The heart chakra is affected by essential oils which promote romance and an overall sense of well-being, such as rose and geranium.

- **The Throat Chakra:** The throat chakra, as one would expect, is located in the center of the throat. This chakra rules over our ability to express ourselves and may require attention anytime we feel as though we are afraid to speak up for ourselves, or on the other end of the spectrum, anytime we find ourselves being untruthful or intentionally manipulating others with our words. Healthwise, this is the chakra that has a direct effect on the respiratory system, so those who smoke or experience allergies may find themselves to be particularly benefitted by working with essential oils geared towards this area. The most common essential oils for the throat chakra are mentholated in nature, meaning that peppermint, eucalyptus, wintergreen, spearmint, etc. are often the top choices.
- **The Third Eye Chakra:** Located in the center of the forehead, the third eye chakra is associated with

clairvoyance and the ability to perceive and move through the boundaries between our world and spiritual realms. Essential oils associated with the third eye chakra, such as juniper, clary sage and heliotrope are meant to increase our receptivity to spiritual energies while removing psychic and mental blockages. The third eye chakra is a particularly beneficial spot for treating restlessness, attention deficient disorder or even the simple inability to focus and concentrate.

- **The Crown Chakra:** Located at the very top of the head, the crown chakra is our gateway to heaven, the communication point between us on earth and the divine realm. This is the chakra that controls our sense of spirituality as well as that which assists us with delving into mysterious realms, such as clairvoyance, etc. The essential oils which are associated with the crown chakra are those that establish a kind of hot-line between our realm and the otherworld, such as frankincense and elemi.

Benefits of Aromatherapy

The National Association for Holistic Aromatherapy defines aromatherapy as an "art and science of utilizing naturally extracted aromatic essences from plants to balance, harmonize and promote the health of mind, body and spirit." Simply put, the aromatherapy is the practice of using essential oils to alter ones physical, mental or emotional state of mind.

Before we get into depth about different essential oils and their individual uses, it is important to understand how essential oils are used in aromatherapy in the first place. There are three primary methods of delivering essential oils to the body. These include inhalation, topical absorption and internal ingestion.

Internal ingestion is by far the most controversial and risky method of using essential oils. While some people think nothing of putting a drop of lemon oil in their daily water bottle, it is important to be aware that very few essential oils have actually been deemed safe for internal use. The bottom line is that the research simply isn't there, therefore the long-term risks are unknown. Unless it is absolutely known to be safe, internal use of essential oils is discouraged, particularly in the cases of children or nursing and/or pregnant women. While it is certainly possible for experts to reap the internal benefits of consuming essential oils, there are far less risky and invasive methods that deliver substantial results, as we will discuss below.

The two most common methods of utilizing essential oils lies in topical or aromatic use. Topical use means that the essential oil is applied to the skin, while aromatic use means that the scent is inhaled via a diffuser or simply worn as a perfume for its aromatic benefits.

Many essential oils are beneficial to the skin in a number of ways. Tea Tree oil, for example, can be applied directly to the skin to ward against ticks, mosquitoes, black flies as well as guarding against funguses like athlete's foot and other contagious conditions. Lavender is particularly soothing to the skin and acts as a natural anti-microbial and demulcent, working to regenerate damaged skin cells and minimizing damage from scalds, burns and overexposure to the sun.

Other essential oils have beneficial topical properties, yet they are too powerful in their concentrated form to be applied directly to the skin. This is where the concept of a carrier oil comes into play. Selecting a good quality carrier oil is essential in the practice of aromatherapy, as the carrier oil is what creates a protective boundary between the concentrated essential oil and one's bare skin. Oftentimes, the most popular carrier oils, such as coconut, jojoba, almond, olive and/or Argon oil carry skin-enhancing benefits by themselves as well, including demulcent and emollient properties.

A number of essential oils are highly valued for their ability to repel insects and ticks. Many of these, such as tea tree, peppermint, juniper and eucalyptus can be freely applied to the skin as long as they are diluted in water first. While more information can be found in the essential oil recipe section, a general rule of thumb is to add anywhere from 10 – 20 drops of essential oil to two tablespoons of carrier oil. Likewise, a lightweight, emergency bug spray that is far gentler for children involves a simple 10 drops of essential oil combined with two cups of water and sprayed on exposed areas of the skin as well as on clothing.

By far, the most popular method of using essential oils in aromatherapy is, as one would expect, aromatically. This means that you are directly inhaling the fragrance from the essential oil in order to access its therapeutic and/or spiritual properties. The most common method of delivering essential oils in an aromatherapeutic environment is via a diffuser. Diffusers are an all-natural counterpart to scented candles, and they carry far more health benefits and less risks with them as well.

Some diffusers are made out of rods dipped in essential oil which travels up the rod and diffuses the scent throughout the room, though the most common and potent diffusers are made out of a small glass bowl that is filled with water and five drops of a particular essential oil before being placed above a burning tea light candle. The heat from the candle heats the water and oil, diffusing the scent throughout the area. Other methods include adding drops of oil to bath water or incorporating them into a massage.

    While aromatic use is by far the safest way to work with essential oils, it is still not entirely without its risks. Particularly if you are nursing or pregnant, be sure to consult your doctor before using essential oils in any form and keep them well out of the reach of children and animals.

The Most Popular Essential Oils

1. **Angelica:** Angelica oil is derived via steam distillation of the seeds. It is a wonderful essential oil for increasing levels of energy, concentration and overall alertness. Diffuse a few drops of the oil throughout a room while studying or reading for increased clarity and focus, as well as for an overall boost in creativity and inspiration!
   Angelica oil is also wonderful for combatting feelings of lethargy and a lack of energy associated with depression and/or anxiety. It can also assist with relieving respiratory issues as well as with lessening the severity and frequency of migraine headaches. Pregnant and/or nursing women should avoid angelica oil in all forms, as it can be toxic to the baby.
2. **Basil:** Basil oil is associated with drawing good luck and prosperity to a home. A few drops of oil diffused throughout an area will help to increase money flow, while inhaling the oil on a regular basis is also believed to stimulate the mood, increase energy levels and promote an overall sense of joy.
   Basil oil is also wonderful for alleviating migraine headaches as well as for encouraging the appetite. It is an effective anti-emetic as well, meaning that it can soothe nausea and upset stomachs.

Basil oil should never be used internally, as it can be toxic and even fatal in the wrong doses.

3. **Bergamot:** Generally obtained via mechanical expression, bergamot promotes a general sense of well-being, joyfulness and child-like gratitude for the moment at hand. This makes it valuable essential oil for those battling depression and anxiety, as well as for anyone with a generalized sense of overwhelming stress.

   On a physical level, bergamot oil has helped with liver and spleen ailments, as well as encouraging the appetite.

   It is however, very important to be aware that bergamot oil is very photosensitive. This means that is can cause irritation to the skin by itself if it is applied with no carrier oil, yet even when the best precautions are taken, it does not react well with direct sunlight. If you are planning on spending time in the sunshine, avoid applying bergamot oil to the skin for at least twenty-four hours before exposure, as severe burns and even blistering can result!

4. **Cedar:** Cedar bark was burned by Native Americans for its ability to purify the spirit and to promote divine protection, and it is used for much the same purposes in modern aromatherapy. Cedar is a scent that is considered to be particularly sacred to the

Gods, thus its aroma is believed to ward against all kinds of evil, including repelling diseases and residual negative energy. Adding a few drops of cedar oil to the corners of a home will cleanse the area of any harmful energies that may be lurking, making this a particularly powerful oil for anyone in need of psychic protection. Cedar oil is also wonderful for improving mental clarity along with promoting wisdom and spiritual awareness.

Medicinally, cedar is a wonderful remedy for mild respiratory ailments, such as bronchitis or seasonal allergies.

Cedar oil is best used aromatically. It can be toxic in some individuals even when ingested in small doses, and it is very irritating to the skin when used topically. Pregnant women should avoid all forms of use of cedar oil.

5. **Chamomile:** Obtained from the steam distillation of the blossoms, chamomile is well-known for its sedative, calming qualities. The oil can be diffused throughout a room to promote restfulness and to guard against nightmares, while applying it topically works to repel insects. According to some folk legends, chamomile oil is considered very lucky, and can attract wealth and good fortune to anyone who anoints themselves with the oil. Washing your hands

in a cup of water that has been mixed with ten drops of chamomile oil is said to encourage monetary flow and professional success, while the oil itself can be used to combat acne, bruising and other skin ailments.

It is interesting to note that those who experience an allergic reaction to ragweed tend to have adverse reactions to using chamomile oil aromatically, so be sure to educate yourself about the potential risks before use. Chamomile oil is not safe for internal use, and any form of ingestion should be avoided unless you are an expert.

6. **Cinnamon:** Cinnamon oil is a very powerful, active essential oil with a number of potent properties. First, it is invigorating, serving to increase alertness and levels of energy. It is considered a very lucky oil as well, working to draw money and prosperity towards anyone who works with the scent. Cinnamon oil not only boosts creativity and overall stamina, it is extremely useful in elevating passion on all levels. This means that it not only increases the libido and draws romantic energy, it can also assist with improving levels of self-confidence and combatting shyness, indifference and/or introversion. Cinnamon oil is very active, which means that it helps to provide speed and intensity to any other oil it is coupled with.

This makes it a very potent addition to essential oil blends which are intended to draw love or money. On a physical level, cinnamon oil helps to strengthen the immune system, and stimulates circulation.

7. **Eucalyptus:** Eucalyptus oil has a powerful, distinctive odor. It is a wonderful oil for students, as it promotes concentration and increases mental clarity. A few drops of eucalyptus oil diffused throughout a room while studying helps with retaining information, as well as with eliminating outside distractions.

   Medicinally, eucalyptus oil is a highly effective respiratory aid. It can also be used as a febrifuge, meaning it can combat fevers by lowering the body temperature when the oil is applied to the chest area. Eucalyptus oil has also shown to be an effective remedy against migraine headaches.

   It is important to note that eucalyptus oil should not be used in any form by those with epilepsy or other convulsive disorders, as it can trigger a seizure. Likewise, women who are pregnant should avoid internal, topical and aromatic use as well. For any individual, internal use of eucalyptus oil is discouraged, as it can be fatal in the wrong doses.

8. **Frankincense:** Frankincense is very soothing, helping to alleviate anxiety and depression while

promoting an overall increase in tranquility. If you ever find yourself in a period of extreme stress, add a few drops of frankincense oil to your bathwater and soak for twenty minutes while visualizing all of your negative emotions melting away. A few drops of frankincense oil on the pillowcase will ensure a restful night's sleep, while also increasing sexual energy.

On a physical level, frankincense is excellent at boosting the immune system, and can be used to keep all forms of sickness at bay! As the oil naturally repels germs, it is a popular natural remedy for alleviating dental issues, such as gum inflammation and gingivitis when mixed with water and used as a mouthwash

9. **Ginger:** Ginger is one of the most versatile, valuable essential oils on the market today. It is powerful and stimulating in nature, meaning that it is wonderful for increasing the libido and overall energy levels while promoting happiness, confidence and an overall sense of self-empowerment!

Ginger oil dramatically improves blood circulation when incorporated into a bath or massage. However, one of the most widely renowned properties of ginger is its ability to soothe nausea and prevent motion sickness. A few drops of the essential oil can be placed on a cotton ball an inhaled for this effect, while a drop or two in a mug of hot water will serve the same purpose. While many pregnant women are able to safely combat the effects of morning sickness by drinking ginger tea or eating small amounts of candied ginger root, it is vital to consult with a doctor before consuming the oil internally if you are pregnant or nursing.

10. **Jasmine:** Jasmine oil is highly beneficial for alleviating stress. Its calming fragrance eases anxiety and banishes depression, making this a highly effective treatment for those who battle with inner demons. A few drops of the oil added to one's pillowcase helps to promote a restful sleep, while wearing the oil topically or adding it to the bathwater is said to assist with drawing romantic energy towards oneself while increasing the libido. Jasmine oil is good for improving mild respiratory ailments. It is also highly effective at treating issues related to female menstruation, such as helping to alleviate cramping. Some midwives swear by diffusing jasmine oil throughout a room as a woman is giving birth to ease labor pains. Although it is non-toxic and one of the safer oils in general, women who are pregnant or nursing should still avoid all forms of use.

11. **Lavender:** Lavender is perhaps the most popular essential oil in the world. It is widely renowned for its multitude of healing properties, both in regards to the mind and the body. Lavender is extremely soothing; therefore, it helps to promote a calm, tranquil environment. Diffusing lavender throughout a room will help to combat stress while promoting a general sense of well-being.

    Lavender promotes restfulness; therefore, it is highly effective in treating cases of insomnia. For children who suffer from night terrors, a few drops of lavender oil on the pillowcase will help to ensure a relief from nightmares while promoting relaxation at the same time. A few drops of the oil can be added to bathwater or simply placed on a cotton ball and inhaled to guard against migraine headaches as well.

    Perhaps one of lavender's most valuable healing properties is in regards to its amazing ability to treat burns and scalds. A few drops of lavender oil applied to the affected as soon as possible after burning helps to not only reduce the pain and prevent against blistering, it dramatically speeds up the healing process as well. This healing quality is so marked that many people keep a small bottle of lavender oil in their kitchen specifically for this purpose!

12. **Lemon:** Lemon oil is uplifting by nature. The oil helps to stabilize mood swings by promoting an overall sense of happiness while increasing levels of vitality and energy. Lemon oil can also assist with improving concentration and maintaining focus. Add a few drops of lemon oil to water for a powerful, all-natural cleaning agent that will fill your house with a delightful fragrance. Lemon oil is a natural anti-biotic, which means that it can help to prevent against disease and illnesses. Adding the oil to one's bathwater is a simple, easy way to boost the immune system, while diffusing the scent throughout the home helps to promote an overall sense of good health and well-being.

    As with other citrus oils, lemon oil is extremely photosensitive. This means that you should never wear lemon oil if you are planning on spending any time in the sun. Even without exposure to sunlight, lemon oil can be very irritating to the skin, so be sure to use a quality carrier oil and conduct a spot test before applying in any sort of volume.

13. **Marjoram:** Marjoram oil is highly effective at alleviating anxiety while promoting a sense of calm and tranquility. If you are feeling overwhelmed by stress, adding a few drops of marjoram oil to your bathwater will quiet your mind almost instantly,

making this a very effective remedy for over-excited children or those who suffer from mania, obsessive compulsive disorder, etc.

Medicinally, marjoram oil serves as a gentle digestive aid, helping to relieve constipation as well as soothing menstrual cramping. It can also help with alleviating mild respiratory issues and increases circulation when incorporated into massage.

14. **Patchouli:** A grounding essential oil that is linked with stability and nature, patchouli oil is widely revered for its ability to increase the libido amongst both men and women. A particularly valuable essential oil for those who find themselves hindered by sexual inhibitions, diffusing patchouli throughout the bedroom or sprinkling it on the bedsheets helps to alleviate any negative baggage one may carry regarding sex, thus encouraging an enjoyable experience for both partners.

    Patchouli oil is also excellent for treating a number of skin conditions. It repels bacteria, acts as an anti-fungal and discourages ticks, mosquitoes and other insects.

    While topical and aromatic use is generally considered safe, patchouli should not be taken internally, as there is no know safe dosage.

15. **Peppermint:** Peppermint is highly stimulating, being used to help increase energy and combat lethargy. Likewise, peppermint oil is valuable for boosting levels of creativity and concentration, as well as promoting an overall sense of mental alertness. Its energy is highly purifying, so it can be diffused throughout a room or area to remove any residual negative energy, or simply put a few drops in your bathwater after a long, stressful day to remove any excess baggage that may be following you around. Inhaling peppermint oil not only boosts energy levels, it can help to quell nausea and prevent motion sickness. Likewise, peppermint oil has been proven to alleviate migraine headaches while also carrying some mild respiratory benefits when applied to the chest. Peppermint oil is highly irritating to mice, spiders and ticks. Place a few cotton balls soaked in the oil in the corners of your home to guard against any unwelcome visitors or dilute the oil and use it on your clothing and backpack during hikes. It is important to note that peppermint oil is highly invigorating, thus it should not be used in any form less than five hours before you are planning on going to bed.

Peppermint oil can be diluted with water for its analgesic and antibiotic effects as a mouthwash as well.

16. **Rose:** Just as jasmine oil is particularly beneficial for women, rose oil is the same. Not only does it help to alleviate feelings of stress, anxiety and depression, rose oil also helps to enhance beauty, attracts love and increases feelings of self-esteem. Diffusing the scent throughout a home is said to prevent against any sort of domestic arguments, while adding a few drops of the fragrance to one's bathwater is said to increase female sexuality and even promote fertility! Rose oil can also be used as a powerful astringent and anti-acne tool. In fact, women are encouraged to mix three or four drops of rose water in with boiling hot water and hang their heads over the steam in order to promote physical beauty and combat the external signs of aging.

17. **Rosemary:** Rosemary oils is one of the most powerful natural mental stimulants currently available on the market. A simple whiff of rosemary oil is invaluable in providing grounding and stability while promoting wisdom and increasing creativity. Students and professionals alike can benefit from using rosemary oil to improve levels of concentration

and memory retention while improving mental clarity.

Rosemary oil is showing promise in helping to preserve the memory of patients with Alzheimer's disease. It also has some pain-relieving effects when applied to tired or sore muscles.

Rosemary oil should not be used in any form by pregnant or nursing women. It should also be avoided by anyone with epilepsy or other convulsive disorders, as well as people with hypertension.

18. **Sandalwood:** Sandalwood oil carries some very strong magical connotations with it. It is believed to assist with opening an avenue to the spiritual realms, promoting wisdom, assisting in acts of divination and promoting an overall strong sense of connection to the divine. For this reason, sandalwood oil is a particularly valuable addition to all sorts of religious and spiritual ceremonies, as it helps to establish a clear connection between the individual mind and the divine. Sandalwood is also heavily associated with sexuality and passion as well. Particularly in regards to men, it restores virility and endurance while increasing levels of passion. Add a few drops of sandalwood oil to the bedsheets in order to loosen sexual inhibitions and encourage erotic play or wear

the fragrance on the clothing to attract the attention of potential female suitors.

On a therapeutic level, sandalwood oil helps to relieve depressive symptoms as well as stabilizing the mood swings associated with premenstrual syndrome. Sandalwood also has sedative and calming properties, meaning that it can be used to promote a restful night's sleep as well. Sandalwood oil can also assist with alleviating muscle tension and inflammation when applied topically. It reduces the severity and discoloration of bruises, and can also combat fungal infections, such as athlete's foot.

19. **Tea Tree:** Tea tree oil is one of the most valuable natural substances in existence. If you decide to work with only one essential oil, tea tree is the most beneficial choice. Not only does the aroma assist with improving mental function by encouraging clarity and boosting creative energies, the medicinal benefits are virtually unparalleled.

Tea tree oil is one of the most powerful topical antibiotics and anti-fungal agents available. Not only does the oil kill germs on contact, it is a powerful repellent for biting insects, such as mosquitos and ticks. Tea tree oil is also a remarkable topical analgesic. It can be applied to fresh stings or bug bites for a numbing effect or use it on ingrown toenails to eliminate inflammation and infection while the nail is growing out.

Lauren Marshall

Quick Ailment Reference Guide - Which oil to use for which problem

If you're ever stuck for which oil to use for which ailment, then just use this chapter as a reference.

Alleviates Anxiety: Angelica, bergamot, chamomile, frankincense, jasmine, lavender, marjoram and rose.

Analgesic: Tea Tree

Anti-fungal: Patchouli, Sandalwood and tea tree.

Anti-inflammatory: Sandalwood and tea tree.

Astringent: Rose

Attracts Love: Cinnamon, ginger, jasmine, rose and sandalwood.

Boosts Creativity: Angelica, cinnamon, peppermint and rosemary.

Clarity: Angelica, cedar, cinnamon, eucalyptus, rosemary and tea tree.

Cleanses the Liver: Bergamot

Cleanses the Kidneys: Sandalwood

Cleanses the Spleen: Bergamot

Combats Depression: Angelica, basil, bergamot, frankincense, ginger, jasmine, lavender, rose and sandalwood.

Combats Migraines: Angelica, basil, eucalyptus, lavender and peppermint.

Cures Bruises: Chamomile and Sandalwood.

Dental Aid: Frankincense and peppermint.

Digestive Aid: Ginger, marjoram and peppermint.

Enhances Divination: Sandalwood

Febrifuge: Eucalyptus

Grounding: Patchouli and rosemary.

Heals Burns: Lavender

Improves Respiratory Function: Angelica, cedar, eucalyptus, jasmine, marjoram and peppermint.

Increases Appetite: Basil and bergamot.

Increases Circulation: Cinnamon, ginger and marjoram.

Increases Concentration: Angelica, eucalyptus, lemon, rosemary and tea tree.

Increases Confidence: Cinnamon, ginger and rose.

Increases Energy: Angelica, basil, cinnamon, ginger, lemon and peppermint.

Increases Sexuality: Cinnamon, frankincense, ginger, jasmine, patchouli and sandalwood.

Laxative: Marjoram

Memory Retention: Rosemary

Menstrual Aid: Jasmine, marjoram and sandalwood.

Natural Cleaning Agent: Lemon and tea tree.

Prevents Acne: Chamomile and rose.

Prevents Nightmares: Chamomile and lavender.

Promotes Good Luck: Basil and cinnamon.

Promotes Happiness: Basil, bergamot, ginger, lavender and lemon.

Prosperity: Basil, chamomile and cinnamon.

Protection: Cedar

Purification: Cedar and peppermint.

Relieves Nausea: Basil, ginger and peppermint.

Relieves Stress: Bergamot, chamomile, frankincense, jasmine, lavender and marjoram.

Repels Insects: Chamomile, patchouli, peppermint and tea tree.

Sleep Aid: Chamomile, frankincense, jasmine, lavender and sandalwood.

Spiritual Awareness: Cedar and sandalwood.

Stability: Patchouli and rosemary.

Strengthens the Immune System: Cinnamon, frankincense, lemon and patchouli.

Wisdom: Cedar, rosemary and sandalwood.

Lauren Marshall

Creating Your Own Essential Oil Blends - 22 Super Simple DIY Recipes

Once you begin to experiment with essential oils, you may become tempted to begin creating your own specialized blends. One of the most important components in creating your own blends is to be sure you are storing them properly. You will need small glass bottles that are not tinted, as exposure to direct sunlight can alter the oil's compounds. Instead, elect for bottles that are dark blue or amber tinted in color.

From here, you want to fill each bottle with approximately two tablespoons of a quality carrier oil, the two best are almond oil and jojoba oil but you can also use apricot kernel oil. This is the base that you will use to construct any of the following recipes. It is important to store these mixtures in a cool, dry area, and be sure to shake them well before using. These essential blends rely on the concept of synergy. This means that one or more essential oils are combined due to their ability to work in harmony to treat a single need. In theory, their combined power is stronger than the single oil on its own.

Some of the most practical, popular essential oil recipes are as follows:

1. **Anxiety Eliminator 1**

    3 drops jasmine

    3 drops rose

    3 drops frankincense

    Add to bathwater each night to promote restful sleep and relief from night-terrors or diffuse throughout the room for an overall sense of safety and well-being. Those who suffer from anxiety attacks may benefit from anointing their clothing with this blend or sprinkling it on their pillowcases and bedsheets.

2. **Anxiety Eliminator 2**

    2 drops bergamot

    2 drops marjoram

    3 drops lavender

    This is a wonderful concoction for eliminating a generalized sense of anxiety in both children and adults. It also assists with promoting happiness and promoting focus, which makes it particularly beneficial for anointing children's school bags and school clothes.

3. **Instant Calm**

    4 drops lavender

2 drops angelica

2 drops marjoram

This is an ideal blend for anyone who suffers from panic attacks. Simply take a small whiff of the blend for instant soothing, or use it in your bathwater at night to prevent against a racing mind or pointless worrying.

4. Nature's Antidepressant

3 drops lavender

2 drops sandalwood

2 drops rose

2 drops bergamot

This is a wonderful oil blend for anyone who suffers from depression, obsessive tendencies or other mood disorders. It helps to promote a gentle aura of happiness when diffused throughout an area, or it can be worn on the clothing as a way of naturally uplifting the spirit.

5. Attracting Love

2 drops jasmine

2 drops patchouli

2 drops sandalwood

1 drop cinnamon

Sprinkle amongst the bedsheet or diffuse throughout the bedroom to increase the libido while lowering inhibitions.

6. Happiness Blend

2 drops bergamot

2 drops lemon

2 drops lavender

Diffuse through a room to promote an overall sense of joy and contentment.

7. Immunity Boost

2 drops lemon

2 drops eucalyptus

2 drops cinnamon

Diffuse throughout the household to promote overall good health.

8. Natural Insect Repellent

4 drops tea tree oil

4 drops patchouli

Mix with three cups of water and spray skin, clothing and bedding liberally to avoid ticks, mosquitos and other pests.

9. Natural Mouse/Spider Repellent

4 drops peppermint oil

2 drops tea tree oil

Use the mixture to soak a cotton ball. Place one cotton ball in all of the areas of the home to discourage pests.

10. **Natural Sleep Aid**

2 drops chamomile

2 drops jasmine

2 drops sandalwood

Diffuse the mixture throughout a room or sprinkle it onto bedsheets to ensure a good night's sleep.

11. **Nature's Housekeeper**

4 drops lemon oil

4 drops tea tree

Place the blend in about two cups of water and mix in a spray bottle for an excellent, all- natural cleaning remedy that is non-toxic and safe for children and pets. Spray on kitchen counters, in the bathtub, toilet, sink or any other area to clean while preventing bacteria and germs.

12. **Sweet Dreams**

4 drops lavender

4 drops chamomile

2 drops jasmine

A simple whiff of this blend before bedtime helps to promote restlessness or diffuse it through the bedroom an hour before bedtime to ensure that children receive a deep, pleasant sleep.

13. Nature's Excedrin

4 drops lavender

2 drops peppermint

2 drops eucalyptus

The best way to use this formula is to simply inhale it at the first sign of a migraine onset. Even if you are not able to use it in the beginning phases, taking a small whiff every ten minutes or so will help to alleviate the worst of the symptoms. Those who are especially prone to stress migraines can combine two drops of lavender to the solution to help promote calmness as well.

14. Nausea Relief

3 drops ginger

3 drops peppermint

Inhale the scent directly from the bottle to alleviate the symptoms of motion sickness, or simply diffuse the mixture through a room to alleviate upset stomachs associated with morning sickness, hangover or digestive issues.

15. Passion Booster

3 drops cinnamon

2 drops rose

2 drops sandalwood

An ideal date-night blend, this is a wonderful addition to a couple's bath or massage, as it arouses the libido and promotes an aura of romance and sexuality. Sprinkle the mixture onto your bedsheet or clothes for the same effect or diffuse the scent throughout a room and watch the sparks fly!

16. Prosperity/Money Drawing Blend

3 drops chamomile

3 drops cinnamon

Use as a hand wash to increase monetary flow or use the oil blend to anoint the purse or wallet for the same purpose. The mixture can also be sprinkled around the house to promote overall good luck.

17. Protection

4 drops cedar oil

Use this mixture to anoint clothing to ward against accidents and other danger, particularly when traveling. This same mixture can be used on objects to prevent them from becoming damaged or stolen. When diffused in an area or sprinkled around the perimeter of a room, it guards against negative energies and wards off any malevolent entities that may be lurking nearby.

18. Bruise Remover

3 drops chamomile

3 drops sandalwood

Mix the oil blend with a cup of cold water and soak a rag in it to create a kind of compress. Drape the cloth over the bruised area for a few minutes to help improve discoloration and to discourage inflammation. Chamomile oil can be very irritating to the skin, so do not attempt this remedy unless you have used it topically before with no adverse effects.

19. Respiratory Aid

2 drops eucalyptus

2 drops peppermint

Mix with a quality carrier oil and rub on the chest for a decongestant effect or diffuse throughout the room or add to bathwater to aid with mild respiratory issues.

20.   The Scholar's Blend

3 drops eucalyptus

3 drops lemon

2 drops rosemary

This is an excellent scent to diffuse throughout an area in order to enhance concentration and help with memory retention. Use it while studying or reading, then carry the bottle with you and take a deep breath of it before a test or exam to boost focus and increase the ability to recall what you have learned.

21. Stress Relief

2 drops jasmine

2 drops lavender

2 drops frankincense

Diffuse throughout a room or add to bathwater to promote an environment of peacefulness, calm and tranquility.

22. Woman's Best Friend

4 drops sandalwood

4 drops jasmine

Diffuse throughout a room or wear as a scent during one's menstrual period for obtaining relief from mood swings as well as to combat cramping and fatigue. This is also an excellent mixture to sprinkle upon the bedsheets to encourage fertility and increase female libido.

Conclusion

And there we go, I hope you've enjoyed this book and that it's proved valuable to you. I urge you to try out some of the recipes listed as well.

One important thing to remember is to only buy high quality essential oils, sometimes cheaper brands pass off "massage oils" as being essential oils - but this is not the case. A surefire way to tell if an oil is fake is if they feel greasy or thick. The exception to this rule is sandalwood, which naturally has a thicker consistency.

Whatever your reason for using essential oils, they are a fantastic, natural way to remedy various ailments, both physical and mental.

Essential oils are quickly gaining recognition for their tremendous healing properties. There is absolutely no question that essential oils help treat the symptoms of different diseases as effectively or more than the drugs which are administered by pharmaceutical companies.

So best of luck to you in your essential oil journey - and I wish you all the best.

Thanks, Lauren

Lauren Marshall

Decluttering Your Home

8 Simple Everyday Minimalism Techniques to Declutter Your Home & Mind - With Meditations for Spirituality, Mindfulness, Healthy Habits and Self Affirmations

By

Lauren Marshall

Introduction

For most of us, living with clutter is simply a way of life. Accumulating possessions is something that we do without giving it much thought. Think about the last time you moved. How many boxes and crates and bags of things did you discover while you were packing that you forgot you even had? How much of this stuff did you choose to keep, for one reason or another, even though you had just rediscovered you had it in the first place? How many times did you look at an object or piece of clothing and decided that you simply couldn't bear to part with it, even though you hadn't worn, used or even acknowledged that it existed in years? Simply put, as we go through life, we accumulate clutter. As the late comedian George Carlin famously quoted in his standup routine, "a house is just a place to keep your stuff while you go out and get more stuff." While this may seem oversimplified, there is a great deal of wisdom in that comical assertion.

Even those of us who like to consider ourselves neat, orderly and organized are not exempt from this tendency. We just conceal it better. Think about it. Everyday, we wake up and go out to do whatever it is that we do in the world. For some of us, this means going to work, while for others, it means raising children, upkeeping a home, attending classes or any other number of activities. Each and every day, no matter what we do, most of us are bound to collect at least one piece of clutter, if not much more than that. At least one piece of paper or magazine will make its way on to the coffee table or kitchen island, never to be glanced at again. Maybe we will find some object in the store that appeals to us for one reason or another, only to purchase it, bring it home, and then promptly forget about it, leaving it to gather dust on the shelf. There might be a tremendous sale at our favorite store, where we will go and purchase things that we kind of like simply because it's a good deal. We might bring home a bag of clothes that aren't really our style and not quite our size, but we simply had to buy them, because it was such a good deal and someone someday might make use of them.

How many of us have a closet or two crammed full of clothes, books and toys that our children haven't touched in over ten years? How many kitchens have shelves lined with dishes that haven't been used since the latest set was purchased, or a cabinet containing Tupperware and plastic containers that are never actually used to store food? How many of us have homes that contain a junk drawer or two, where we toss all of the odds and ends we pick up throughout the day? How many of our bathroom cabinets are lined with half-used personal hygiene products and/or cosmetics we used once or twice and didn't really like, but for some reason, can't bring ourselves to throw it in the trash? Even after we no longer have a need for the possessions we have accumulated, we tend to stubbornly hold on to them.

There are a number of reasons for our refusal to let go. Maybe we don't want to get rid of any piece of artwork our children ever painted or any article of clothing they ever wore when they were a baby simply because we are trying to hold onto the child that they once were. Maybe we don't want to throw away the brochures, maps and travel guides from our latest vacation because we somehow think that if we do so, we might not remember the experience as well. Maybe we keep notes from our high school friends and movie ticket/concert stubs and other random memorabilia with the vague idea of creating a scrapbook someday.

While the urge to collect clutter is certainly common, it is also ultimately detrimental to our mental and even physical well-being. The constant accumulation of possessions can make the entire ambiance of our home chaotic and unorganized, rather than the welcome respite from the outside world that it is intended to be. Likewise, holding onto too much stuff can actually harm you physically, as it creates a breeding ground for dust and mold, along with creating potential fall hazards and blocking routes of escape in case of an emergency.

The aim of this book is to help the reader understand how decluttering and minimalism can greatly improve your life.

Lauren Marshall

In the following pages, we will farther explore the connection between clutter and the effect it has on the mind and bod. We will also explain how ridding yourself of clutter and unnecessary possessions helps to provide a liberating effect, and also improves concentration and promotes relaxation. The first part of this book delves into the connection between your physical surroundings and your state of mind/being. It explains the reasons behind why we constantly accumulate clutter, and introduces the concepts of decluttering and minimalism. We will learn practical ways to remove clutter from our home to create an environment that promotes serenity and contentment. The second part of the book introduces the concept of mindfulness, and how it is related to eliminating clutter. Here, we will learn about meditation and different techniques that we can use throughout the day in any situation to help alleviate stress and anxiety.

Chapter One: The Importance of Decluttering and Minimalism

In 2014, Japanese author Marie Kondo released her book titled The Life-Changing Magic of Tidying Up: The Japanese Art of Decluttering and Organization. Widely heralded as the decluttering Bible, her book has since gone on to be a New York Times Bestseller, with over seven million copies sold worldwide and having been translated into over thirty different languages! Kondo's popularity doesn't stop there, however! She has a waiting list for personally consulting clients that wraps around the block, as well as bearing the title of being one of Time Magazine's 100 most influential people. This book is widely based around the Japanese concept of the value behind decluttering and minimalism.

Simply put, decluttering refers to the process of getting rid of all of our unnecessary possessions. Minimalism is about achieving freedom through simplicity. In today's consumer culture, it is very easy to become caught up in the game of accumulating possessions. From a very young age, most of us are taught that in order to be successful and happy, we must acquire a car, a house, and then fill said house with all kinds of possessions. In much of the world, the possessions we have directly reflect our status, thus we accumulate as much as we can as fast as we can, just so that everyone knows how important we are. Even when these possessions are no longer useful, we loathe to part with them, just in case we may somehow find a use for them again someday. Minimalism teaches us that by no longer allowing our possessions to define our worth, we are able to achieve greater freedom and liberate our minds from thinking we must cling to every possession we have ever had. Instead of focusing upon the material things surrounding us, minimalism places emphasis on finding happiness via exploring life, interacting with loved ones and most of all, by focusing upon creating a state of mind that makes you happy.

Why Do We Accumulate Clutter?

Generally speaking, there are three major reasons why people tend to accumulate and hang onto clutter. These are related to feelings of nostalgia, perceptions of future utility and appreciation for beauty and quality.

Let's tackle the big one first. Nostalgia is hands-down the most common reason people resist against decluttering. Our hearts and heads often have very different priorities, and nowhere is this discrepancy more apparent than in the concept of decluttering your home and life. Of course, we still have the lock of hair from our daughter's first haircut hidden away, along with the first tooth she ever lost and the birthday candle from her first cake. Same goes with an article of clothing, handwritten note or other possession that was once the property of a loved one who is now deceased. Even though we may never actually take these keepsakes out and look at or appreciate them, we get a strange sense of comfort just knowing that we have them. As is the case with a huge number of our possessions that have become clutter, we have an emotional attachment to these objects. They are keepsakes of a person or moment in time that we wish to remember and keep with us forever. On some sort of level, in our heads we fear that if we were to get rid of these things, we will somehow lose our connection with the person it represents to us. Throwing away these keepsakes equates to throwing away precious memories, and this is something that we naturally resist against. In almost every instance, nostalgic clutter is by far the easiest to accumulate and the hardest to let go of.

Another reason why we tend to hang onto clutter is out of the pervasive belief that perhaps, someday, we may have a need for every object we have ever acquired. Maybe you haven't lived in an area where snow accumulation is a viable possibility for over two years, yet you still refuse to part with the down jacket and winter boots stashed away in the closet, just in case a rogue blizzard was to suddenly hit town. Even if our own children haven't played with the board games and stuffed animals tucked away in the attic for over a decade, we hold onto it, just in case our younger sibling or cousin decides to have a baby one day, and might want to make use of it. College textbooks sit on the bookcase, accumulating dust, yet we spent good money on those books, and you never know, someday there might be a need for a refresher course in calculus. As humans, we have a natural tendency to want to be prepared for every situation. We cling to the possessions we acquire, storing them away in attics, basements and closets with the idea that they are there waiting for us if the need for them ever arises. Most of us were also raised with the idea that wastefulness is bad. Therefore, we feel that if we throw away the things that we or someone else paid good money for, we are wasting that money.

Finally, we sometimes accumulate and hold onto clutter for aesthetic reasons. While the stained glass lamp our sister-in-law bought us for a Christmas present four years ago may not be our style, the sheer beauty of the lamp makes us feel as though we must put it on display and keep it in our homes. The sheet set we bought because it was such a good deal may never actually be used on the bed, but we can't bear to part with it, because they felt so soft in the store and we know they are of a high quality. For those of us who collect things, this is an area where hanging onto something purely because of its visual appeal can cause clutter to become out of control. Even if we know we do not need more porcelain dolls, model airplanes, paintings or whatever it is we collect, we will continue to purchase and hoard these things out of habit, and because we know that a new addition will look so pretty next to all of its counterparts.

One of the first steps in deciding to declutter your home is to identify which of these three categories the majority of your clutter falls into. Once you have a true understanding as to why you accumulate clutter, you will be in a better position to honestly evaluate your attachment to your possessions. For instance, for those of us who collect clutter for nostalgic reasons, we must begin with a psychological shift that allows us to accept that letting go of objects does not mean we are letting go of memories or our loved ones.

How Does Clutter Affect Our Health?

Even though we may think that the objects which make up the clutter we accumulate brings us comfort, status and security, multiple studies have shown that keeping clutter around can actually have some very serious side effects on both the mind and the body. As humans, we are conditioned to want to hold on to everything we have, yet clinging to our possessions can cause us serious harm. Let's examine some of the ways that clutter can adversely affect us.

Lauren Marshall

Clutter can contribute to higher stress levels

A recent study conducted at the University of Los Angeles found that having clutter lying around the home or office can significantly increase stress levels, particularly in women. Everything from dirty dishes in the sink to an ever-mounting stack of laundry to wash, fold and dry to an explosion of papers strewn across the desk can make it very difficult for us to truly relax when we come home at night. Likewise, a work space that is constantly cluttered markedly contributes to a sense of stress and discontentment.

The presence of clutter raises the stress hormone cortisol in our brains. This, coupled with the excessive visual stimulation that accompanies a cluttered environment can cause us to feel anxious, irritable and perpetually on edge. Every time we walk into a room, we are reminded of all the work and cleaning that needs to be done. If we want to have friends over for dinner and drinks, preparing for what should be a happy event becomes extremely stressful as we race around the home to make it look clean and organized.

Clutter can cost you money

Paper is an enormous source of clutter, even in today's paperless, email-driven society. Most of us have at least one area in our homes that acts as a landing zone for every piece of paper that comes through the door, whether it be junk mail, coupons, fliers, renewal notices, bills, etc. When all of these papers are kept in disorganized piles rather than being neatly filed and systematically thrown away, it is very easy to lose track of important financial documents. We might forget to pay our cable bill until we start getting phone calls because the actual bill has been buried under a mountain of other papers since it first arrived in the mail three weeks ago. We might have to pay a ticket because our car has been unregistered for over a week, simply because the renewal form got lost in the chaos and was forgotten.

It is not only misplacing or losing things in the clutter that can have an impact on our finances. When we have so many possessions laying around in multiple places, it can be very difficult to know exactly what we actually have. Take for example the simple activity of hanging up a few pictures in the family room. You know that somewhere in the house, you have nails and a hammer, but after spending half an hour searching, still can't seem to locate either one. You go to the hardware store, buy the tools you need, and come home to hang the pictures. The hammer and unused nails promptly disappear into the void of clutter in the basement, meeting the same fate as their predecessors. Say that a week later, you need to hang another picture. Again, you can't locate the tools you need, so you go out and buy them *again*. In a home without clutter, you would know exactly where to look. There wouldn't be a waste of time hunting things down, as the tools would be placed back in the same location each time immediately after being used.

Clutter decreases focus and lowers levels of concentration

Have you ever woken up with a clear list of things you'd like to accomplish that morning? Say that your goal is to go for an early jog and cook yourself a healthy, hot breakfast before jumping in the shower and sprucing up a little before you have to leave for work. You've planned it out so you'll be ahead of the traffic, with fifteen minutes to settle in and get comfortable before your first meeting. You feel ready to take on the day as you hop out of bed. It takes you a minute to find your shoes (they were under the bed), and while you're tying them on before headed out the door, you realize that the roll of plastic wrap is still sitting on the kitchen counter from the night before. You pause for a moment and walk over to put it away, and noticing that there are a few glasses and plates in the sink, stop again to rinse them and load the dishwasher. The rubber bone you trip over in the front hallway reminds you to stop and fill dishes with food and change water bowls, and the shirt hanging over the back of a chair must go into the wash before you can begin the day. You finally make it out the door, and have a brief reprieve of relaxation while jogging, but as soon as you get home and check the time, you realize that your way behind schedule.

You want to cook something for breakfast, but the refrigerator is in such a state of disarray you can't find the ingredients you need for anything besides coffee and cold cereal. On your way to the shower, you pause to collect a few of the kid's toys and put them back in their proper place. By the time you actually get yourself in the shower, you have just enough time to put together a single outfit from your overflowing closet and jump in the car, only to barely arrive on time.

The presence of clutter distracts us from what we are trying to do. By ultimately eliminating the cutter we have in our everyday surroundings, we eliminate the majority of the distractions we face every day. Without a multitude of unfinished tasks staring us in the face at each moment, we are able to quickly accomplish exactly what we set out to do.

Clutter can make it hard to breathe

The more objects we have, the more we open the door to those things accumulating dust or even growing mold. The presence of mold or dust in the environment can have significant negative effects upon the respiratory system. Those who live with clutter run the risk of compromising their immune system, leading to an increase in everything from the common cold to influenza and even pneumonia. People with an already compromised respiratory tract, such as those who suffer from asthma, COPD or allergies are particularly susceptible to the detrimental potential side effects of a cluttered environment.

Clutter can literally cost you your life

Most of us have seen television shows which showcase individuals who have taken accumulating clutter to the extreme form of hoarding. In some of these cases, people find it virtually impossible to part with anything, thus, they end up living in a home that has every surface covered with papers, boxes and all other kinds of possessions. You cannot move easily through the hallways. You cannot access or open the windows and doors. And yet, what the majority of people do not realize is that we don't have to go to the extreme of hoarding for our clutter to present a serious potential issue to our personal safety. Large stacks of paper or other flammable materials present a definite fire hazard. The fall hazard presented by disorganization is very real as well, as is the possibility for potential emergency exits being compromised in the moment they are needed the most.

Clutter can compromise your sense of well-being

The connection between the mind and body is well documented, and very real. If something negatively impacts our brains and emotions, that same thing has the power to likewise manifest negatively in the body. When we live in a home with clutter, our personal lives feel more cluttered and chaotic as well. When our workspace is cluttered, we often find that we have a hard time focusing and moving forward at work. According to the principles of Feng Shui, a Chinese practice that stresses the harmonization of energetic forces throughout the home, clutter is nothing more than wasted space that constantly sucks away and blocks energy. Once the clutter is removed, beneficial energies have the opportunity to move freely, which opens the gateways for contentment and satisfaction.

Chapter Two: Freeing Yourself from Clutter

Perhaps today is the day that you decide to make a change. Making the decision to be an active participant in the decluttering process is certainly first and arguably the hardest step. The thought of methodically sorting through all of our possessions and ruthlessly tossing aside all but the most functional/favorite initially seems cold, unfeeling and even unnatural. We may feel an initial moment of panic, worried that we will be parting from things that we carry attachment to, for whatever reason. And yet, as intimidating as the process may seem at first, the vast majority of people who choose to declutter their homes experience higher levels of happiness and contentment as a result. Some people delight in the fact that everything in their home now serves a purpose or brings happiness, while others appreciate the more practical aspects of decluttering, meaning the home is far easier to keep clean and organized.

If you have decided that you are interested in decluttering, it is important to go about the process the right way. It can appear to be very overwhelming, or even impossible at first. Below is a list of steps that can help you prioritize your possessions and mindfully restore order and control to your life.

Step One: Set realistic expectations

Unless you are going to immerse yourself one hundred percent in a strict minimalistic lifestyle, there will never be zero clutter. This is a simple fact of life and one that needs to be accepted. If you are raising young children, it is virtually impossible to immediately put everything back in its place every time. And you certainly don't want to waste the magic and wonder of their younger years by obsessively worrying about messes. In some instances, we must acknowledge that we can only do the best we can in terms of keeping clutter at bay.

Step Two: Take a deep breath

Yes, the initial though of decluttering your home is scary. Even though you know you don't need all the stuff taking up space in your closets and basement and attic, on some sort of primal, emotional level, our hearts still skip a beat at the thought of parting with it. This is when it is particularly important to understand the reasoning behind we accumulate and hold onto clutter. Once we understand the motivations behind a behavior, it is much easier to look at it in a rational, realistic manner rather than allowing it to mindlessly control our behavior.

Step Three: Get everyone on board

Even if you are wholeheartedly dedicated to decluttering your home, the process is not going to work if your spouse comes home every night with an armload of junk mail and leaves his shoes in the middle of the kitchen floor. If your roommate is bringing things into the apartment as fast as you can mindfully move them out, you are fighting a loosing battle. In order for the decluttering process to truly work, everyone in the household must be on board and on the same page.

Step Four: Take it one room or category at a time

The worst thing you can do in the beginning stages of the decluttering process is to self-sabotage. If you wake up one morning and decide that you are going to somehow declutter your entire home by sundown, you are almost certainly setting yourself up for failure. Odds are, you have been in your home for at least some period of time, and in keeping with human nature, you have accumulated possessions accordingly. Rather than putting pressure on yourself to do too much too fast, break the process down into small, manageable chunks.

Set yourself a goal each day, and accomplish it. Some people like to work one room at a time, meaning one day they tackle the clutter in the bedroom and another day, tackle it in the kitchen. Other people prefer to declutter their homes by category. This means one day, you might make the choice to go through and declutter your books and magazines, while another day, you might focus on clothing or children's toys.

Step Five: Touch, ask, acknowledge and decide

Say that it is your first day of the decluttering process, and you are taking on your first room or category. First and foremost, keep in mind that decluttering is supposed to be a cathartic, empowering activity rather than something that is traumatic or stress-inducing. The idea is to make the purging process an enjoyable, mindful moment rather than increasing anxiety. So, don't be in a hurry, and don't put too much pressure on yourself. Go into the task with an open yet firm mindset. As you go through the first room or category, let your own inner voice be the guide for what you should keep and what you should let go. One of the best ways to do this is through first physically touching and examining the object. Use all of your senses, if you can. Feel its texture in your hands, take in each detail with your eyes and breathe in its aroma. Once you have thoroughly examined the object in your hands, take a moment, and honestly ask yourself if whether or not that particular object brings you joy or serves an active purpose in your life. If the answer is yes, keep it in a place of honor and enjoy its presence daily. If the answer is no, put it aside. If you truly can't remember the last time you wore that beautiful red dress you bought on vacation years ago, it is probably time to let it go. Yes, you may have paid a lot of money for it, and yes, it reminds you of a wonderful point in time, but the reality is, it doesn't do much besides hang in your closet anymore.

This does not mean that you are expected to coldly toss your once beloved possessions in the trash as soon as you've decided you no longer need them. Giving thanks is an important part in the decluttering process. Acknowledge the role that this particular possession has played in your life, and the place it holds in your heart. It is certain that some things will carry too much sentimental, practical, material or aesthetic value to part with, but those things should be few and far between. Keeping one or two of your most treasured artifacts from your children's baby days is fine, but an entire box? Probably not. This is where you must be ruthless, and decide whether or not you truly need the object you have in your hands. If the answer is not an immediate yes, joyfully release the object and let it go, confident in the knowledge that someone else may have an actual need for it.

Step Six: Create a maintenance plan

The tendency to accumulate clutter is insidious. Once you have gone through the decluttering process, it is important to keep your guard up and formulate a plan to ensure the continued organization and serenity of your home. One of the simplest yet most commonly overlooked ways to keep clutter at bay is to get into the practice of immediately putting things back where they belong. Instead of walking through the door at night and tossing your keys on the counter and your jacket on the back of the couch, take the extra time to hang everything up where it belongs. It seems such an insignificant step, but having everything in its place goes an unbelievably long way to creating an orderly, serene environment.

Another major way to prevent clutter from piling up is to come up with a system. Instead of allowing papers to pile up, get in the habit of going through the mail and other papers each and every day. Promptly throw out anything you do not have a need for, such as junk mail. For the things you may want temporarily, such as a magazine or grocery flier, it is ok to hold onto it just long enough to read it, after which, it needs to be sent on its way. For the few and far between papers you do actually need to keep, such as bills and important documents, file these neatly away in a spot that allows you quick access without constantly being in your line of vision.

The bottom line is that you need to come up with a maintenance plan for minimizing clutter that works for you. Some people like to live by the rule of one-in, one-out. This means that if you make the choice to bring something new into the house, such as an article of clothing or book, you must balance the new possession's presence by getting rid of something else. Other people strongly benefit from picking a set date, be it once a week or month to dedicate entirely to walking through each room in the home and removing any possessions which are no longer necessary. As long as it yields the results you want, there is no truly right or wrong way to keep clutter accumulation at bay.

Chapter Three: The Importance of Mindfulness and Meditation

What is Mindfulness?

Simply put, to be mindful means to live in the moment. It means being aware of your surroundings and taking in what is going on around you with all of your senses, and not allowing yourself to be sidetracked by anxiety or other emotions. While this may seem simple, remaining mindful in today's hectic world is a great challenge indeed. When we are in a mindful state, we are able to objectively and fully observe what is going on around us. Likewise, we are then able to appreciate our surroundings to their fullest extent, and can respond to people and situations with objectivity and wisdom rather than blind emotion or instinct alone. To be mindful means that we are fully present and engaged in the moment we are experiencing. We only take in what is happening now, rather than allowing the moment to be overshadowed by demons from the past or insecurities about the future.

There are two basic tenants of mindfulness – staying in the moment and reserving judgment,

Staying in the moment means exactly what is sounds like. Particularly if we are a naturally a little high strung, the concept of being present in the moment and not worrying about the past or future can be a little intimidating. Yes, we all can agree that it would be fantastic to be able to only focus upon what is happening immediately in front of us, but there are many different variables, such as children playing in the next room, pets scampering about outside or any other number of things that make it very difficult to keep our mind in the present moment. This is where it is important to have a true understanding as to what it really means to be fully present in the moment, and mindful. Mindfulness does not ask us to forget about our responsibilities and obligations. It is not a simple philosophy of out of sight, out of mind.

Instead of worrying about what could possibly be wrong and fretting that we do not have enough, mindfulness teaches us the value of appreciating what we already have. When we stop comparing our lives and possessions to others and learn to see the value of the things already surrounding us, we find it much easier to want to be present in the moment. Instead of worrying that we will not have enough resources to fend of potential disaster someday, we are able to rest assured that we have all we need for now, and can take contentment in knowing that that is enough in and of itself.

The second major aspect of achieving mindfulness is reserving judgment. Instead of instantly judging a person or situation as good or bad, we instead take the time to consider the possibility that everything happens for a reason. For example, if we fail to achieve a certain goal, such as landing a particular job, getting into a certain college or winning the affections of a certain someone, we may be tempted to fall into a state of despair, beating ourselves up over what we perceive as a failed result. And yet if we to are consider the same problem from a standpoint of mindfulness, we realize that we have not failed. When we reserve judgment and focus upon living in the present moment, it is much easier to accept that each perceived failure conceals some sort of hidden lesson. Yes, the job you went after may have gone to someone else. Yes, the man or woman you shamelessly wooed last weekend may be stepping out without someone else the next day. The test you prepared so meticulously for might have included questions that your notes couldn't groom you for.

Does this mean that you failed? Absolutely not. This is where reserving judgment comes into play. Do not judge your recent breakup as being good or bad, instead simply accept it as something that happened, acknowledge and honor it, and then move on. It does us absolutely no good to dwell upon the guilt and/or regret associated with the past, just as it is equally useless to obsess and worry over the future. At each and every point in your life, you are perceiving what is happening in the present. To pay attention to anything else distracts from the concept of mindfulness.

Being mindful is a mental state that may require some form of practicing to achieve. Most likely, we have grown up in a consumer culture, and have therefore been taught that our possessions make up our status and reflect who we are. We are also taught that we must constantly be vigilant of downplaying our past and grooming our future to ensure the best life possible. We think that we must judge, compete against and outshine others in order for our own worth to be evident. When we make the choice to move towards choosing mindfulness, we willingly and joyfully let go of every regret from our past along with any anxiety regarding our future. Instead, we focus upon making the absolute best out of every moment as it presents itself to us.

There are a number of different ways to encourage a state of mindfulness. These include participation in daily prayers, getting into the habit of morning affirmations and/or statements of gratitude as well as an increase in physical activity, such as taking up yoga, jogging or any other sport that helps you focus your energy. Yet multiple studies suggest that one of the quickest ways to make mindfulness an everyday part of life is through regular participation in some sort of meditative process.

The Three Types of Meditation – And Which One is Right for You

Meditation is a technique that is used to cultivate mindfulness. The practice of meditation alters one's state of mind, bringing an elevated sense of consciousness along with improving focus. Meditation is ancient, transcending throughout many different cultures and religions from all over the world. While meditation is most commonly associated with the Buddhist and Hindu religions, it is also practiced in Judaism, Christianity and Islam as well.

There are countless ways that people choose to meditate. However, almost all meditative practices fit into one of three categories, concentrative, mindfulness or guided meditation.

Concentrative meditation is concerned with achieving the highest state of being possible. As the name implies, here the emphasis is on complete and total concentration. Most of the time, the practitioners elect to place all of their focus upon their breathing, though others prefer to concentrate on the repetition of certain words of phrases which make up a mantra.

Mindfulness meditation is less concerned with concentrating on something specific and more geared around achieving a state of mindfulness. Here, the practitioner utilizes meditation to promote a greater awareness of the here and now. Mindful meditation places emphasis on being present in the moment and opening oneself to experiencing their surrounding with an open, non-judgmental mind. This form of meditation is particularly beneficial in alleviating stress along with anxiety and depression.

Guided meditation involves one or more people taking part in a meditation session that is verbally led by a trained practitioner. This teacher actually acts as a guide, providing you with auditory input that influences the act of meditation. Guided meditation usually happens in a face to face environment, yet it is also effective through recorded audio or even simply via reading a text. Guided meditation is very useful in helping someone resolve an issue through the meditative process. The guide helps to construct a meditative session that is tailored to the individual's particular need. For example, if the person meditating has been struggling with grief, the guide may gear the session in such a way that the person is led through a mental exercise in which they are able to release some of the pain and begin the process of letting go. Guided meditation is very successful in clinical practice, helping alleviate symptoms of anxiety and depression.

Hidden Benefits of Meditation You Never Knew About

Meditation can reduce levels of anxiety and stress

Regular participation in meditation can actually help us train our minds to experience less stress and anxiety. By utilizing what is called the relaxation technique, the practitioner combines concentrative and mindfulness meditation. The relaxation technique involves focusing upon and repeating a singular word in order to bring ourselves into the present moment. By repeating the word and focusing upon existing only in the here and now, the body achieves a sense of serenity and calm. If we practice the relaxation technique enough, it is easier to train our bodies to go into a relaxed state when we are faced with external stressors.

Meditation can increase levels of self-awareness

Many times, when we are faced with a stressful situation, our minds automatically revert to old habits and coping mechanisms. Rather than immediately responding with increased levels of stress and anxiety when a challenge presents itself, meditation helps us stop and honestly evaluate the situation. When we learn to take a moment and reflect before reacting emotionally to a problem, we find that we are able to take on that situation with greater wisdom and clarity. Regularly practicing meditation helps us increase self-awareness by helping us to stay in the present. Achieving this mindful state reminds us that we have dealt with difficult situations before, and survived to tell the tale.

Meditation is good for your health

Not only does meditating boost the immune system, it alleviates physical ailments that result from carrying too much stress and tension around. Thus, regular meditation can decrease blood pressure, help us sleep better and can even help us lose weight, as we tend to be more mindful as to what we are putting in our body.

Meditation improves our memory and helps us concentrate

The practice of meditation involves going within oneself and remaining still. This is easier said than done in the busy world that we live in. By regularly giving yourself time to simply sit and focus upon being in the moment, it becomes easier to focus upon the task at hand when dealing with our day to day tasks. The mounting to do list that greets us at the beginning of each day can seem overwhelming when we look at everything we need to get done. Yet, if we are able to break the list down into smaller steps and simply focus upon achieving one goal at a time, the process does not seem as daunting.

Meditation can help improve our relationships

Studies have shown that people who engage in regular meditation are naturally more empathetic. When we focus only upon getting through the day, it is easy to lose track of the fact that we are surrounded by others who's needs and desires are just as significant as our own. Meditation opens us up to a sense of universal consciousness, meaning that we become more aware of our place in the world as a whole rather than thinking of ourselves as a singular, lone entity. When we are able to pick up on the emotional needs of others and treat them as seriously as we would our own, a greater sense of understanding is achieved. A behavior that would normally spark irritation or anger, such as not feeling as though our significant other is listening to us, is instead treated as an opportunity to learn what that person is trying to tell us by their actions.

Some classrooms have begun to replace punishment with mindfulness. This means that an infraction that would normally land a student in detention instead results in time spent in mindfulness and meditation. These schools have found that they experience a dramatic decrease in problem behaviors, such as acting aggressively towards other students or refusing to focus upon the task at hand. Rather than focusing solely upon punishing the student, meditation instead gives the student the opportunity to relax, regroup and focus upon their own behavior and how it affects others.

Meditation can boost levels of creativity

Many writers, entertainers and artists find that they receive some of their best inspiration through the process of meditation. It provides us with a space to clear our minds of anything unimportant, thus allowing the inspirational juices to flow freely. Many people who regularly meditate actually create a sacred space inside their heads which they visit frequently. Within this space, we not only find increased levels of confidence and contentment, but also open ourselves us to receiving inspiration.

Meditation enhances spirituality

Whether or not you consider yourself religious, participating in meditation helps to put you in touch with a higher power. Spirituality involves getting in touch with our inner selves, and meditation helps us do this. By creating a quiet space in which we can simply be still, we are able to better focus our intentions and open ourselves to the subtle energies surrounding us.

Meditation can help combat negative behaviors

While meditation is something that anyone can do, it does take practice. Learning how to block out outside distractions and simply focus upon the moment is more difficult than it sounds, particularly if we have been raised to believe we must constantly be doing or accomplishing something. Meditation forces us to develop self-discipline. This self-disciple coupled with the cultivation of a safe, serene space inside our minds can be extremely helpful in combatting addictions or other self-destructive tendencies.

Meditation can decrease physical pain levels

We all suffer from physical discomfort from time to time. For most of us, we choose to just grin and bear it, ignoring the signs our bodies are giving us and pushing through with the day's tasks. Meditation not only helps us slow down and listen to the cues our body provides, it has also been shown to actually stimulate the areas of the brain which are responsible for numbing physical pain.

How to meditate, even if you've never done it before in your life...

While there are countless different approaches and methods for meditation that you can choose to learn from, the truth is that there is no singular right or wrong way to do it. Some people insist on constructing all sorts of formal rules and regulations around the practice, believing that you must engage in meditation first thing in the morning. Others think that there must be a certain kind of incense, music or other tools present to achieve the desired results. Meditation is a very personal process. If you get the best results first thing in the morning, then by all means, this is when you should meditate. Likewise, if having music playing softly in the background helps you, keep that music playing for as long as you'd like.

But what if you can't meditate early in the morning, because you need to get up and get your kids ready for school before you go to work? What is music playing in the background is a distraction, and burning incense doesn't do anything other than give you a headache?

The best meditative ritual for you to establish will be to figure out what works for you, and to do it. Don't worry if someone else says its wrong, or insists you should be doing it differently. Although there are no absolute rules when it comes to meditating, there are a few general guidelines to help you get started.

Step One: Remove yourself from any distractions you can

Finding a quiet place where you will be free from interruption is harder than you may think. Even if you manage to steal away for a few moments, there is still the phone going off constantly or a toddler calling your name just outside the door. No matter how much we may wish it to be different, life does not stop and start at our convenience. Thus, it is important to find a time and place for meditation that works for you. Even with the best laid plans, recognize that there will be times you are interrupted, and that is okay. The goal is to try to set yourself up for a distraction-free environment the best you can. Pick a time when you are alone in the house with at least fifteen or twenty minutes to spare. If there is no one else present that can demand your attention, the only one who can present a distraction is yourself.

This is where you need to prepare accordingly. Leave your phone in a different room, or if you insist on having it with you, turn it off or at the very least, silence it. With the exception of a true emergency, there is nothing that is going to happen in this time you are taking for yourself that can't wait for a response. Even better, after engaging in meditation, you will be better prepared to react to any situation with mindfulness rather than blind emotion. We all love our pets, but this is a time when it is probably better to close the door, as you don't want to reach a relaxed state only to have the cat jump into your lap or the dog lick your face!

If you live with other people where alone time is virtually impossible, don't be afraid to speak up for yourself. Tell your roommates that you need a little while by yourself, and ask them not to disturb you unless it is absolutely necessary. Explain the importance of what you are doing for yourself to your spouse and ask them to keep the children occupied so you have a moment to center yourself.

Step Two: Prepare your mind and body

Yes, you can meditate anytime, anywhere, as we will see later on. With that being said, there are certain things that you can do to ensure that your body and mind are in the best state possible to achieve mindfulness.

First of all, the importance of getting enough sleep cannot be overstated. Most people find that they function best when they get anywhere from seven to nine hours of sleep each night. Too little sleep can leave us with difficulty concentrating and an overall cranky disposition, while too much sleep is just as harmful, resulting in depression and lethargy. Strive your best to go to bed at a reasonable time and likewise, make the effort to get up and get going at a decent hour as well.

Second, it is best to only engage in meditation when you are not under the influence of alcohol or drugs. While it may seem as though having a few drinks or engaging in other recreational drug use would help with relaxation and expanding the mind, keep in mind that the goal of meditation is to achieve clarity and mindfulness. By definition, drugs and alcohol have an effect on our state of consciousness, making it ultimately harder to achieve the state of focus we are after.

Step Three: Get comfy

It is very hard to relax when you aren't comfortable. You want to be sure that you pick a space which has a soft, padded space for you to sit, whether it is a cushion, a specific mat or simply plush carpeting. Likewise, don't dress in anything that is constricting, as you want to be able to breathe freely and focus upon the moment, not how itchy your shirt is. Check the temperature to be sure it is what you like before you begin as well.

Some people have a specific room or area in their home that is dedicated solely to the purpose of meditation. They cultivate an environment of beauty and sacredness in this area, preparing it with only the things that bring them the greatest sense of joy. While it is certainly not realistic for everyone to have a meditation room, you do want to try to create a sacred space for yourself. This means clearing the area of any clutter and surrounding yourself with the things that make you happy, whether it be a bouquet of fresh flowers, an animal figuring or the joy of smelling your favorite candles burning. Get rid of anything that makes you feel anxious, sad or angry, at least for the purpose of while you're meditating.

Step Four: Have a seat

Sit in a position that is comfortable, and rest your hands so the palms are facing up. Some people prefer to lie down while they meditate, and this is fine, as long as you are able to not fall asleep!

Step Five: Breathe and focus

For the first few minutes, simply sit and breathe normally with your eyes closed. As your breath starts to fall into a rhythm, focus upon that rhythm and slowly start to breath deeper and slower. This will naturally help you begin to relax. Try to focus your mind only upon your breathing. If you start to get mentally sidetracked, just pull yourself back to thinking about your breath.

Step Six: Visualize

Meditation helps us all create our own special place that we can turn to in times of turmoil for guidance and wisdom. Oftentimes this area that lies within us gets gradually built up over time and with each session of meditation. If you are just beginning, once your body feels fully relaxed and you are focused only on your breathing, allow yourself to envision a space that speaks to you on a soul level. For some people, it is a sandy tropical beach or wooded forest while for others, it might be as simple as a room. Whatever mental setting makes you feel content and joyful is the one to develop as time goes on.

Some people elect to participate in guided meditation. This involves an outside source providing clues during the meditative process. This is a particularly good tool for those who are new to meditation, as it helps to develop visualization skills.

Chapter Four: 8 Exercises for Everyday Mindfulness You Can Do at Home...with no extra cost

Exercise One: Experience food on every level

Take a piece of your favorite fruit, whether it be an apple, banana, cherry, peach, mango or strawberry. The goal is to experience this fruit fully by focusing your senses. First, feel the fruit in your hands, whether with your eyes closed or open. Feel the texture of its skin – is it smooth or bumpy? Fuzzy or naked? Tough or soft? Second, take the fruit in with your eyes, observing every detail you can, from color to any blemishes that may exist. Third, smell the fruit and experience any memories you may have associated with that aroma. Finally, bite into the fruit and taste it fully. This is an exercise that can be done with almost any food, not only to help us have a greater enjoyment of each meal, but also to keep our brains focused on the immediate moment.

Exercise Two: Relax yourself bit by bit

Sit or lie down in a comfortable position. Begin by regulating your breathing, then focus on each part of your body individually, feeling it relax as you go along. For example, begin by focusing upon your toes and feeling each one relax before moving on to your ankles, foot, lower legs, upper legs, hips, etc before finally arriving at the top of the head. This helps us to hone our focus by forcing us to concentrate on one area of the body at a time while still relaxing the system as a whole.

Exercise Three: Take it all in

If you live in an area where the weather is permitting, dress yourself comfortably and head outside. Find an area you are naturally drawn to, and make yourself comfortable. Simply sit and be in the moment, taking in anything that you see. This could be anything from simply watching a cloud pass over the sun or leaves falling in the autumn wind to a squirrel gathering nuts or even a fellow wandered making their way by. The point is to sit in stillness and fully take in what is occurring around you without making judgments. Try to look at things only as they are, without reading anything else into it. If something in particular draws your focus, such as bird flitting from branch to branch, absorb yourself in the experience as much as you are able. This exercise helps us learn how to fully take on what is going on around us without harboring expectations and/or judgment.

Exercise Four: Train your thoughts

Our thoughts have an incredible impact upon our minds, and therefore, our experience of reality. The undeniable power of positive thinking has been long acknowledged by psychiatrists and scientists alike since Dr. Norman Vincent Peale released his book pf the same title in 1952. Following the simple rule of like attracts like, we understand that if we have negative expectations regarding a situation, we are far more likely to experience those same negative aspects than someone who greets the problem with an optimistic mindset.

This exercise helps us train our brains to replace negative thoughts with positive ones. It involves constant vigilance, meaning that we must actually think about what we are thinking. Anytime we catch ourselves thinking something negative, such as "I'll never be able to get that done," or "I can't do anything right," we immediately replace it with a positive, empowering thought. Instead of convincing ourselves that we won't ever be able to study enough to get a good grade on our final exam, we instead focus upon the steps we can take to ensure that we will do the absolute best that we can do. The longer we engage in this exercise, the easier it becomes, as our brains can actually re-wire themselves to think positively rather than negatively.

Exercise Five: Find your happy place

This is a simple, easy technique for cultivating mindfulness that can be done quickly and in nearly any environment. If you find yourself faced with a stressful or emotional situation, take a few minutes and try to calm yourself as best as you can. Once you are relaxed, close your eyes and recall one of the happiest memories you have. It can be a place you once visited, a person whose company you immensely enjoy or any other number of things, as long as it brings you an intense feeling of joy and contentment. Picture this favorite place, thing or person in your head as clearly as you can, soaking in all of the positive energy the vision supplies you with. Then simply open your eyes and go about your day with a renewed focus and energy.

Exercise Six: Work with a guide

As people get into the regular process of meditation, many find that they establish a connection with some sort of internal guide along the way. This guide can appear in many different forms, although most commonly, it is another person or some sort of animal. If the idea of working with a spirit guide appeals to you, try the following exercise.

Once your breathing is regulated and you are fully relaxed, ask your guide to appear to you in your minds eye. Do not try to force anything, and do not pass any kind of judgment on any visual input you may receive. Simply note what happens, and keep practicing this technique for as long as you need to before you are able to establish a rapport with your guide.

Exercise Seven: Surround yourself with light

This is a quick, easy exercise that can be done nearly anytime and in anyplace. If you should find yourself feeling overwhelmed, anxious or stressed out, find a quiet place you can escape to for a minute. This might mean retreating to the bathroom at work, or shutting yourself in a room at home. Once you are alone, shut your eyes, take a few deep breaths and visualize a soft blue light surrounding you. See this vision as clearly as you can in your mind's eye, and as you watch the light envelop you, release whatever tension it is you are carrying. Allow this light to encircle you, bringing comfort and serenity. As you get ready to end the session, visualize yourself drawing the light into yourself. When you open your eyes, you will feel a dramatic increase in contentment and peace.

Exercise Eight: Stress in, stress out

This is a good way to take five minutes out of your day to release any negative emotions and regain a state of mindfulness. Find a comfortable spot to sit for a moment, and focus on your breathing. Once your breathing has become regular and deep and you are feeling relaxed, begin to visualize. Picture any stress, sadness, anger or other negative emotion inside of you as a grey smoke that leaves your body every time your exhale. As you breathe in picture a brilliant white light swirling around you and enter your body. This white light collects inside of you and builds up until your whole body is glowing and sparkling, as each bit of grey inside of you is expelled. Once your entire body is filled with light, slowly picture that light condensing itself in your center, between where your heart and hips are. As this light grows smaller, see it become concentrated into a pure ball of positive energy. Hold this image for a few breaths, and then slowly count to ten to re-center yourself.

Lauren Marshall

Other books by Lauren Marshall

Hemp Oil and CBD: Your Guide to Using Medicinal Oils for Physical Injuries, Mental Health & General Wellbeing

www.ingramcontent.com/pod-product-compliance
Lightning Source LLC
Chambersburg PA
CBHW071453080526
44587CB00014B/2094